BY THE EDITORS OF
CONSUMER GUIDE®

PRACTICAL GUIDE TO
CAT
CARE

Sheldon Rubin, DVM

Publications International, Ltd.

CONTENTS

EMERGENCY CARE

About the Author: Sheldon Rubin, DVM, is a practicing veterinarian in Chicago, Illinois. He received his Doctorate of Veterinary Medicine from the University of Illinois and served as President of the Chicago Veterinary Medical Association. He is a member of the American Animal Association, the American Veterinary Medical Association, and the Anti–Cruelty Society.

Cover Photo: Seide Preis Photography

Introduction

Cats and people have traditionally had a relationship curiously full of contradictions. In the course of their journey through the ages, cats have been loved, hated, put to work as rat catchers, feared as agents of witchcraft, and honored as sacred creatures. Thousands of years of history lie behind today's domestic and household cat.

Some people claim that the cat—unlike the dog—has never completely accepted domesticity. But it's just that quality of independence that many owners find so endearing (and challenging) in their cats. And cats are wonderful companions. They're intelligent, self-possessed, affectionate, and loyal. They're very adaptable—equally at home in a mansion or a small apartment. They're clean (fastidious, in fact) and easy to care for. They're beautiful to look at and highly entertaining.

These traits make a cat the perfect pet. And, in fact, so deep is the friendship that can exist between a person and a pet that scientists have given it a name—the human/companion animal bond.

What does your cat ask of you in return for its companionship? Food and shelter, certainly. Grooming, perhaps. Routine health care. Medical care if it's necessary. And, of course, your friendship and affection. This book tells you how to care for your cat, from choosing the sort of cat that will be happy in your household to knowing what to do in an emergency.

CHOOSING THE RIGHT CAT FOR YOU

Cats have been on earth for more than 50 million years, long before the earliest dogs appeared on the scene. Evidence suggests that the Egyptians were the first people to domesticate the cat, and archeologists have uncovered Egyptian tombs in which embalmed cats were buried alongside their masters. It's believed that the first cats were brought to Europe by the Phoenicians around 900 B.C., and that the Romans were responsible for bringing the cat to England. The Egyptian cat thus traveled far beyond its birthplace and is the ancestor of the domestic cats we know today.

In the course of history, cats have been both worshiped (with temples built in their honor) and hated and feared as devils. In the Middle Ages, cats—particularly black cats—were associated with evil spirits, witchcraft, and devil worship. A witch's cat was looked on as her "familiar" who aided her in witchcraft and was often destroyed along with her. It's likely that this association of the cat with the witch and her night-time craft gave the cat its reputation for being "sneaky."

Apart from its more dramatic associations with the powers of both good and evil, the cat has a long work record as a killer of rats and mice. The Europeans certainly used the cat for this purpose, and it appears that the white settlers from Europe brought the first domestic cats to North America. These colonists also put the cats to work keeping down the mice and rat population.

The cat is a carnivorous meat-eating animal with teeth designed to grasp, hold, and break up prey in the wild. A cat cuts and tears its food rather than crushing and grinding it. In the wild state, however, the cat eats the entire prey—bones, organs, and all—and in this way gets a balanced diet. The domestic cat that gets only selected parts of the animal can't live on meat alone and is a meat and vegetable eater.

One of the most attractive qualities of the cat is its cleanliness, and for this it can give most of the credit to its unique tongue. The cat's tongue is coated with multiple small barbs that it uses for grooming; they keep it exceptionally clean. The cat also has keener sight than most domestic animals and sees quite well at night. The shape of the cat's eyes is a throwback to its wild ancestors and their after-dark hunting activities. Even the most domesticated cat may still sleep all day and go out on the town at night.

Cats And People: Comfortable Friends

The cat makes a delightful pet. Although very independent and requiring little care, a cat offers wonderful companionship in any type of environment, from high-rise apartment to country estate. And companionship is the major reason why people own cats. Despite their independence, cats are highly affectionate and love to be petted, stroked, and fondled. They take care of themselves with the utmost skill and are highly entertaining. Because cats are so adaptable and easy to care for, they make ideal pets for bedridden or elderly people who would be unable to provide the care and exercise needed by a dog.

As a result of scientific research, there is now medical evidence to prove that the company of a cat can do some people more good than sophisticated medications. Scientists have discovered that Americans who own a pet live longer than those who don't, and that in the act of petting a cat, a person's blood pressure drops.

Elderly people in nursing homes who seem to have lost the will to live can be brought out of their shells by having a cat or dog to touch and relate to. Children with learning disabilities or behavioral problems often improve dramatically when a pet comes into their lives. In fact, children and older people benefit to such a degree from owning a pet that cats and dogs are now used in therapy by psychologists and psychiatrists.

Another reason for getting a cat—a purebred, in this case—is because you want to breed it. Unfortunately, as any good breeder can attest to, breeding cats is a monumental job with little or no profit involved.

If your cat is a mixed breed, you should, as a responsible pet owner, think twice before letting her have kittens. America has a vast over-population of cats, millions of which are homeless and either die from one cause or another or have to be destroyed in humane shelters each year. Anyone who wants a cat will have no trouble finding one—from an animal shelter or elsewhere—and nobody who cares about animals wants his or her cat to breed indiscriminately and add to the miserable army of unwanted animals that roam across the country.

If you do decide to get a purebred cat for breeding purposes, you'll almost certainly want to exhibit the cat in shows. Breeders enter their cats in shows in the hopes that they will gain points that will eventually add up to championship status, thus increasing the animal's value for breeding purposes. The best way to get started in cat showing is to join a particular breed club.

Whether you want a purebred aristocrat or a mixed breed, remind yourself that even though cats are so easy to live with, any cat will make certain demands on you—long-term demands, at that. A cat will cost you time, energy, and money. Cats need food, shelter, and routine medical care—vaccinations, for instance. They get sick and sometimes need specialized care that can be expensive. You'll need grooming equipment, a litter tray (which you'll have to keep clean), and perhaps a harness and leash. If you travel, you have to take the cat along or make special arrangements to have it cared for.

Remember, also, that it's always a mistake to get a cat "for the children" and to expect them to be responsible for looking after the newcomer. Although having a cat is undoubtedly beneficial for

children, you must be sure the children are mature
enough to treat an animal properly.

Another thing: Remember that owning a cat is a
long-term commitment. A healthy cat may well
live 15 years or more. So that adorable kitten
playing with the kids will still be around when the
kids are in college or off on their own. And it'll still
be your responsibility.

The Nitty-Gritty Questions

So do you *really* want a cat? If you've taken a
good look at the long-term responsibilities of cat
ownership and decided that you're willing and able
to take them on, there are still a few practical,
nitty-gritty questions to answer:

Do you want a male or female cat?

Do you want a long- or short-haired cat?

Do you want a purebred or mixed-breed cat?

Do you want a kitten or an adult?

Take them one by one. Each is an either/or
question, and in the last three there are specific
advantages and disadvantages to each alternative.

Do you want a male or female cat? The sex of
the cat you want to buy is largely a matter of
choice. Neither sex is healthier than the other. As a
general rule, females are cautious, gentle, and quiet.
Spayed (neutered) females are probably the most
pleasant cats to have around, and you don't have to
contend with the female's heat cycles during which
she, and neighboring males, are very vocal. Unneutered females are prone to uterine infections,
breast tumors, and—of course—pregnancy.

Male cats are larger than females and are more

outgoing and curious. Neutered males are gentle and very active. Unneutered males tend to spray urine (to mark their territory) and to roam and get into fights. Males are susceptible to cystitis (bladder infection) and subsequent plugging of the penis with tiny stones.

Do you want a long-haired or short-haired cat? The answer to this question depends largely on how much work you're prepared to put in on your cat, and—if you want a purebred cat—on the type of breed that takes your fancy. Long-haired cats are glamorous, but it's your job to keep them that way. A long-haired cat will require you to put in a lot of time on grooming to keep it looking good and to keep the hair from becoming knotted and matted. Also, long-haired cats shed a great deal and you must be prepared to put up with having cat hair all over your home. Long-haired cats get hairballs more frequently than short-haired cats. (Hairballs are accumulations of fur that pass into the cat's stomach when it grooms itself.)

If you or a member of your family is allergic to cats, the long-hair vs. short-hair question is virtually decided for you. Because long-haired cats shed more than short-haired cats, they're less suited to an allergy-prone household. If you or a family member has a severe allergy, the Rex cat, which sheds very little, is probably the only practical cat to consider.

Note that an allergic reaction to cats differs from an allergic reaction to dogs. In the case of dogs, the allergy is caused by dander—dried flakes of skin that fall off when the animal sheds. Although it's

CLASSY CATS

If you're looking for a cat with class, the following are some of the pure breeds you can choose from. These are the 10 most popular breeds in the United States today, according to the American Cat Fanciers' Association.

PERSIAN *(Long Hair)*
Glamorous long-haired cat. Distinctive pushed-in "Peke" face, which is the result of over a hundred years of careful breeding. Gentle. Intelligent. Not good with small children. Requires daily grooming.

MAINE COON *(Long Hair)*
Traditional American breed dating back to the early 1800s. Shaggy coat. Quiet. Intelligent. Good with children.

SIAMESE *(Short Hair)*
Exotic, streamlined cat. Blue eyes. Distinctive cream-colored body and darker "points" on face, ears, tail, legs, and feet. Standard colors are seal point, blue point, lilac point, and chocolate point. Temperamental. Very social. Loves human companionship.

ABYSSINIAN *(Short Hair)*
Thought to have descended from the cats of ancient Egypt. Looks like a miniature cougar. Gentle, affectionate, and playful. Very intelligent and loyal. Soft, resilient coat that's easy to care for.

EXOTIC SHORTHAIR *(Short Hair)*
Persian in type and temperament, but with a shorter, plush, easy-to-care-for coat. Quiet. Affectionate.

SCOTTISH FOLD *(Short Hair)*
Descended from Tayside Region of Scotland. Rounded, short, muscular body, with a dense short-haired coat. Ears are folded forward and downward.

ORIENTAL SHORTHAIR *(Short Hair)*
Sinuous and sensuous with emerald eyes. Long, tubular body with a swanlike neck and large, flared ears. Very loyal.

AMERICAN DOMESTIC *(Short Hair)*
Basic, domestic, mixed breed cat. Loyal family pet for hundreds of years. Medium to large cat with short, thick coat. Very hardy. To be a show cat, must conform to one of about 30 recognized colors and patterns.

BIRMAN *(Long Hair)*
Originated in Burma, where it was considered sacred. Strongly built, elongated and stocky. Long, silky hair. Four white paws. Gentle and playful, yet quiet.

BURMESE *(Short Hair)*
Descended from the cross between one cat imported from Burma with a Siamese. Medium build but heavy for the size. Short, glossy coat. Affectionate. Very active.

commonly believed that the cat's dander similarly causes an allergic reaction in a susceptible person, recent research suggests that the actual allergen may be the cat's saliva, which is deposited on the fur during grooming.

Do you want a purebred or mixed-breed cat? If you want a cat that you can exhibit in shows, then obviously you're looking for a purebred—the actual process of choosing one will be discussed later. Purebred cats are more expensive than mixed breeds—they can be *very* expensive. The rarer the breed, the more expensive it becomes; so if you want the prestige of owning a cat that's a class act, you'll have to pay for it.

Don't, however, make the mistake of buying a cat just because it's unusual. Find out all you can about the breed first. This is not hard to do, because years and years of selective breeding have given cat fanciers a good idea of what to expect from a certain breed in terms of appearance, character, health considerations, and longevity. But there's a catch: Indiscriminate breeding and inbreeding have produced cats that are not representative of the breed. It's essential, therefore, to buy a purebred only from a reputable breeding establishment or cattery, and to know what you're looking for before you buy. The breed chart in this chapter shows some of the most popular purebreds and describes some of their prominent personality traits.

Apart from status, however, there's no difference between a cat with a pedigree and a cat that's a mixture of all sorts of breeds. You may find, in fact, that a mixed breed has inherited the best of all its ancestors, and may be sturdier and longer-lived than a purebred.

Choosing between a kitten or an adult cat can be an emotional decision. Kittens are cute. *All* kittens are cute. If you have kids, they'll probably beg you to get a sweet little kitten. Remember, though, that you're not buying the cat just for the children; as mentioned earlier, the cat will probably still be around when the children are long gone. And it's always a mistake to succumb and get a pet for a child who absolutely promises to take care of it all by himself or herself. Trying to make a child take on full responsibility for a pet never works. It's unfair to everyone—the child, the cat, and you. When you're tempted, remember the huge number of cats that undergo euthanasia in humane shelters, or that wander the streets without a home. A lot of them started out as kittens some youngsters promised to take care of all by themselves. Don't take any chances that the little kitten your kids talk you into buying will sooner or later wind up among the pathetic army of cats nobody wants.

Whether you choose a kitten or an adult cat should depend on the amount of time and patience you want to expend. Having a kitten around is very rewarding and a lot of fun, but it does take up a lot of your time. The big advantage of starting with a kitten is that a kitten will fit easily into the family routine, whereas an older cat takes much longer to adjust.

An older cat brought into the house may be a

product of somebody's problems; that cat certainly deserves a home, but be prepared for some social-ization problems that will need some work to straighten out. A well-adjusted, fully grown cat, however, may offer its new owner less to worry about than a kitten. It may already be neutered, vaccinated, and litter trained and may need only to find a nice bed—like yours—to curl up on.

If you'd rather avoid the lively kitten stage and get an older cat, it's a good idea to go to a rep-utable animal shelter or humane society. There's no shortage of cats available for adoption, and you'll be giving a home to a cat that might otherwise be destroyed. Although you'll know nothing of the cat's background, the shelter should be able to alert you to any problems the cat may have as a result of past mismanagement or abuse. But don't assume all shelter animals have problems; many have no problems beyond the need for a home.

Selecting Your Cat: The Do's And Don'ts

Let's assume you've decided to get a cat and you have some idea about the kind of cat you'd like to share your home with. You're ready to buy your cat, but don't rush into it. Here, as elsewhere, impulse buying can get you into a lot of trouble. Where you get the cat from is as important as the type of cat you get. If you're looking for a purebred cat, go to breed shows and talk to owners. Buy cat magazines and study them, or go to the library and read up on the different breeds. Look on bulletin boards in grocery stores. Visit the local pet shop. Check the advertisements in your local newspapers. Ask around. Call the local veterinarians. Visit humane shelters and observe the physical environment (it should be clean and pleasant) and the condition of the animals.

You can acquire a cat from one of several sources, the most common being a private owner, a cattery, or an animal shelter. Whichever source you choose, certain basic rules and safeguards apply, and there are signs that can alert you to the fact that a source is less than reputable. You shouldn't go far wrong if you keep in mind the following do's and don'ts:

• *Don't* buy a kitten before it's six weeks old—the ideal age is eight weeks. Kittens that are removed from the litter too soon often develop strong attachments to people but don't get along with other cats. Conversely, the longer a kitten is deprived of affectionate human contact, the longer it'll take to adjust to people later on.

• *Don't* buy from any establishment that is not clean and orderly, or where the cats seem listless and out of condition. Unsanitary surroundings breed unhealthy kittens.

• *Don't* buy from a "mill"—a place that seems to be full of kittens of many different types.

• *Don't* buy from any owner who won't let you come into the house to inspect the cat, or won't let you spend time alone with the cat.

• *Don't* buy from any owner who seems reluctant

17

r your questions or provide a detailed
al history of the cat.

• *Don't* accept a cat from an owner who won't
give you an unconditional guarantee that, if your
veterinarian finds something wrong with the cat in
the first two or three days after purchase, you can
return the animal for a full refund.

• *Don't* believe anyone who tells you that a kitten
under four months old has had "all its shots." It
can't be true.

• When you're choosing from a litter, *don't* choose
a kitten that looks weak or thin, and *don't* choose
one that's shivering in a corner—even if you feel
sorry for it. It's the "runt," or weakest of the litter,
and it may never grow into a really healthy cat.

• *Don't* accept a kitten that has diarrhea; it can be
the sign of parasites or other health problems.

• *Don't* choose a kitten that is sneezing, or has a
runny nose or runny eyes. It probably has an upper
respiratory infection.

• *Don't* choose a kitten that has patches of fur
missing. This could be a sign of ringworm (skin
fungus).

• *Do* check on the reputation of the establishment
you're getting the cat from. Ask your veterinarian
or, if you're buying a purebred, check with the
breed club for that type of cat. (Breed clubs are
organizations of people with a special interest in
one breed of cat, and they know all the main
breeders in the country.)

• *Do*, if at all possible, observe a kitten's parents and check out their temperaments. Aggressive parents often breed aggressive kittens, although the temperaments of kittens in the same litter can be as different as night and day. The environment you provide for the kitten will also have a lot to do with molding its personality. However, seeing the parents will give you a 50 percent chance of predicting what to expect as the kitten grows up.

• If you're buying a purebred kitten, *do* be aware of any hereditary defects the breed is susceptible to; if you've done your homework, you'll know what they are. Ask the breeder if a veterinarian has checked the kitten for these hereditary defects.

• *Do* be impressed by the professional or home breeder who has these checks completed routinely before offering kittens for sale, and who encourages you to have the kitten examined by your veterinarian immediately after purchase. Any reputable breeder will give you the option of returning the cat if your veterinarian finds anything wrong in the early days.

• If you're buying a purebred cat, *do* be sure that the breeder gives you any necessary registration papers and a copy of your cat's pedigree (family tree). Note that a pedigree is, in itself, no guarantee that your purebred cat will do well in cat shows. Basically, all the pedigree tells you is that for three generations the kitten has come from purebred stock. A good breeder who knows you're buying the cat for show purposes will not, however, sell you a kitten that doesn't reveal promise of becoming a good "show specimen." Breed clubs are closely knit enclaves where everyone knows everyone else, and the breeder's reputation is on the line. So it's clearly in the breeder's best interest to sell only kittens that will do credit to the cattery's name.

• If you're getting the cat for your family, *do* take the whole family along to see how the cat reacts. If you have young children, ask the owner how the cat gets along with children and how it reacts to a lot of excitement.

• If you're buying an adult cat, *do* spend a few minutes with it away from its owner; this will give you a chance to estimate how willing the cat is to make friends with someone new. This opportunity to check each other out is particularly important when you're getting a cat from a shelter and have no knowledge of its parentage or past beyond what the shelter staff is able to tell you from its own observations. Make allowances for the cat that may have had less than happy experiences and may be shy or nervous.

• Above all, *do* ask as many questions as you want. A reputable owner or breeder who's anxious to place an animal in a good home will be more than glad to answer all your queries. Any reluctance to answer questions or to let you see the environment is a sure sign that you'd do better to look elsewhere.

YOUR CAT
BECOMES ONE
OF THE FAMILY

You have now made some decisions about your cat: You know if you want a male or female, a cat with long or short hair, a purebred or a mixed breed, a kitten or an adult. You've looked into various sources and decided where to get your cat. Now's the time to do some practical preparation for cat ownership. Here's what you need to do before you bring the newcomer home:

• Brief the family on how to treat the newcomer.

• Arrange a place where the cat can be confined comfortably until it's trained (unless you're sure it's already litter trained).

• Make sure this area is as cat-proof as possible: Hide electrical cords and remove glass objects and any other items that can be easily broken or knocked over.

• Be prepared to provide appropriate food and water.

• Buy a collar with an identification tag and, if you plan to take the cat out of the house, a harness and leash.

• Check on local licensing requirements and regulations that affect cat owners.

21

• Locate a veterinarian and introduce yourself to him or her.

The arrival of a new pet is always exciting, especially when there are children in the family, but too much action and emotion will disturb and confuse the cat. Remind everyone that overexcitement will panic the cat, that a kitten tires easily just like a baby, and that a grown cat will need time to adjust to a new environment. If you have children, remind them that you're not going to let them carry the kitten around and display it to all their friends—not at first, anyway. For one thing, an animal is not a toy and a kitten is small and easily hurt. For another, a kitten will squirm a lot because it's insecure, and may squirm right out of a child's arms and fall.

The correct way to lift and hold a cat is demonstrated in the illustrations on pages 113 and 114. Slip one hand under the animal's chest so that the chest is resting in your palm. Then lift the cat firmly toward you so that its body is secured between your forearm and your body. Grasp the top of the front legs with the fingers of your right hand, which is still supporting the chest.

If you have other animals, it may be smart to let the kitten or cat adjust to the environment for a few days before exposing it to these pets.

What will the newcomer eat? The amount of food that your cat or kitten will require each day will depend on many factors, of which activity, age, environment, and sex are just a few. Balanced commercial cat foods are readily available and are very easy to use. There are three types: canned (which has the highest water content), semi-moist, and dry. Types of cat food are discussed further in the chapter on nutrition.

Where Will Your Cat Sleep?

Training a kitten or cat to sleep in one place is almost impossible. You can train it not to sleep with you by removing it from your bed—repeatedly, if necessary, until it gets the message. Cats, however, tend to sleep wherever they want to: on top of a dresser, under a bed, or in a closet. A new kitten should be confined in one room with its litter box; in the beginning, it will sleep in that room. The only way to keep it in the room is by closing the door.

If you want to encourage the cat to stay out of the laundry hamper or linen closet and sleep in its own bed, you can choose from a wide variety of cat beds and baskets. However, all you really need is a cardboard box with fairly high sides; cut one side down so that the cat can get in and out easily, and line the bottom of the box with towels or other comfortable cloths. Be careful to keep the cat out of drafts.

The first few nights that a kitten spends away from its litter mates can be traumatic for it, and for you. It helps to tuck a hot water bottle into its bed and to set a ticking clock or a quietly playing radio nearby; these surrogates will take the place of the warmth and sounds of the litter and help it feel less lonely. If the kitten cries the first few nights, be patient. Don't give in and let it sleep in your bedroom or on your bed; you'd be setting a precedent you may not be happy with later. After a few nights, it'll quiet down and be content on its own. The same goes for the older cat—although in this case you can dispense with the hot water bottle and the clock.

Litter Training: The Clean Cat

One of the major conveniences of owning cats is that it's so easy to train them to use a litter pan in the house for urinating and defecating. A litter pan should be made of a nonporous material—stainless steel or plastic, for example. You can either buy a litter pan at a pet shop or use something as simple as a plastic dishwashing pan. The most common litter material is commercial clay litter and you need only two to three inches of litter in the pan. After using the pan, the cat will scratch at the litter to cover the soiled area.

Solid wastes should be removed with a scoop daily, and the litter material should be changed completely at least twice a week. To control odors, sprinkle baking soda on the bottom of the pan before putting the litter in, and wash the pan thoroughly with soap and water before you put in clean litter. After handling the litter pan, you should always wash your hands; a disease called toxoplasmosis can be transmitted to humans through contact with the cat's feces. Toxoplasmosis is discussed in the section on internal parasites (page 103).

Training a new kitten to use the litter pan is probably the easiest task you'll have. Simply place the litter pan near where the kitten is going to eat and sleep. After the kitten has eaten, place it in the litter pan and let it play around for a while. Soon you will see it dig a little, sniff around, and then eliminate. If you catch it eliminating anywhere but in the pan, pick it up immediately and place it in the pan; it will soon get the idea. While you're training the kitten, it's a good idea to leave a small amount of feces in the pan even when you change the litter. This will help the kitten remember what the pan is for.

Although most cats are very clean creatures, occasionally you meet one that breaks all the rules. And a cat that won't use the litter pan can be a real problem. Some cats will defecate in the pan but urinate elsewhere in the house. Some will urinate in the pan and defecate somewhere else. Some cats will defecate and urinate right next to the pan but not in it. Other cats choose to use a rug, a couch, a shoe, a plant, or a chair and will eliminate repeatedly in that one place. Yet others will void wherever they please.

New kittens are seldom the culprits, unless a previous cat marked the rug or couch with urine so that the odor lures the kitten away from the box. In such a case, it's necessary to have the carpet or couch cleaned or removed.

Male cats that are not neutered will urinate out of the pan, and will mark their territory by spraying urine on furniture, walls, and doors. Male cats will also urinate out of the pan if they have cystitis. Signs that the cat has cystitis are small spots of urine around the house, or blood-tinged urine in the sink or bathtub; often times the cat will howl and strain to urinate. (Cystitis is discussed on pages 199–201.) Female cats that have not been spayed will often urinate out of the pan when they are in heat, or like male cats, if they have cystitis.

A very popular alternative to the litter pan for some cats is the soil around a houseplant. The easiest way to deal with this is to get rid of the plant or hang it from the ceiling.

The list of instances of inappropriate urination and defecation can go on and on, but treatment is a very individual procedure. Unneutered cats that are not using the litter pan should be neutered. Any cat that has cystitis needs immediate veterinary attention. If a previously clean cat has suddenly stopped using the pan, you need to determine what is bothering it. It could be something as simple as your having moved the litter pan or started using a different type of litter. It could be that the cat doesn't think you're keeping the litter clean enough. The cat could be upset by a lot of commotion in the house, or jealous of the new baby. Sometimes you won't be able to find the answer, and the solution may lie in putting a number of litter pans around the house, especially in the areas most subject to the cat's misdirected attentions. It may even be necessary to confine the cat to one room until it seems to have gone back to using the litter pan; this may take weeks or even months.

The problems that can cause a cat to soil your home are many, and the solutions are few. It is very important, however, to differentiate bad behavior from illness. Any time a cat breaks litter training, your veterinarian should give the cat a complete physical examination and do a urinalysis and fecal analysis.

Should The Cat Go Outdoors?

In a high-density urban setting, it is not advisable to let your cat outdoors where it will be in contact with strays and be exposed to disease and fights. In a rural area, or if you have a fenced-in yard, you may decide it's safe to let the cat out. Cats do enjoy the outdoors—it is, after all, their natural environment—and love to play in the garden and stalk birds and squirrels. If you are going to let your cat outside, there are several rules to follow:

• Walk with your cat and keep it on a leash and harness.

• Be certain your cat is wearing a collar and identification tag in case it gets lost.

• Be certain your cat's vaccination schedule is up to date.

Remember, however, that a cat can live happily without going outdoors. Cats make wonderful indoor pets, and your apartment or house can be a great play yard and provide all the entertainment your cat needs. You should, however, cat-proof your home—both for your own sake so that the cat doesn't destroy things you hold dear, and for the cat's sake so that it doesn't come to harm. First, hang, protect, or dispose of all plants that the cat can get into.

Some cats are very aggressive with their front claws, and they claw your furniture and drapes to shreds. Cats scratch in order to sharpen their nails and to get exercise, so if you'd rather the cat didn't use your best armchair for this purpose, introduce it to a scratching post. You can buy a scratching post (some are quite elaborate) at the pet shop, or make one yourself by covering a solid wooden post with coarse carpeting. This way you'll save yourself a fortune in upholsterer's bills. Remember, though, that it's very important to introduce the kitten to the post when it is young. You may have to take the kitten to the post and put its front feet on it, as if scratching for it. Sprinkling catnip around the base will help lure it to the post. It should soon figure out what you want it to do. In some cases, no matter what you do, the cat will still prefer your couch or chair, and you may need to have the cat declawed. (Declawing is discussed later in this chapter.)

If your cat is an indoor cat, you should be aware that it depends on you for its social life, so you need to be extra generous with your attention and affection. You can also provide toys to keep your cat amused.

All healthy cats, especially young ones, are curious and playful and love playing with toys—it's very entertaining to watch them, too. You can improvise toys for your cat very easily so long as you select things that can't be pulled apart or swallowed. A simple toy such as an empty thread spool attached to a heavy string and tied to a doorknob can give your cat hours of enjoyment. A catnip mouse can keep a cat happy for months, and most cats love batting a large rubber ball with their paws.

Introduce new toys slowly and watch to see what your cat's favorite playthings are, but be careful to avoid potential hazards—like loose bits of string or yarn that aren't attached to anything. And put your needle and thread away after use. If your cat swallows it (and it might), it will have to be surgically removed.

The Legalities Of Owning A Cat

Besides being a good neighbor and doing everything possible to prevent your neighbor from disliking your cat, you are obligated by certain laws to carry out certain tasks. Most communities have leash laws that apply to cats as well as dogs and that require the cat never to be off a leash when outside your property. Rabies vaccinations are becoming mandatory in more and more areas of the United States, and some communities require that you license your cat as well as your dog. The cost of the license frequently helps support the local animal pound. You can call your local city hall or municipal building for information on legal requirements in your area.

Leashes And Grooming Aids

The type of basic equipment you need—there's not much of it, in any case—depends on whether you are going to let your cat go outside or not. Sooner or later, however, you will need each of these items:

Collar and leash. In many areas, particularly urban areas, you are legally required to keep your cat on a leash. In any area, your cat should have a collar with an attached identification tag. If you are going to keep the cat indoors or only let it go outside in your company, a regular cat collar and harness with identification is all that is necessary. If you are going to let the cat outside on its own (which is not recommended), you should get a collar that has an elastic band built in; if the collar gets caught on something (a branch, for instance) while the cat is jumping, it will slip off rather than trap and strangle the cat.

Brush and comb. A short-haired cat needs to be brushed with a medium-stiff brush. A long-haired cat should be combed before brushing. The best equipment to use is described in the chapter on grooming.

Nail clippers. If you have not had your cat de-clawed, clipping its nails may spare your furniture a lot of damage. Don't ever use human nail clippers on your cat. You can get special cat nail clippers from any pet supply store. If you don't know what to get, ask your veterinarian.

Cat carrier. A cat carrier is a must for every cat owner. It's a container, usually made like a wide-bottomed suitcase, with a carrying handle, plenty of ventilation holes, and sometimes a peephole or window. Carriers come in many styles. Some have a clear plastic or wire mesh upper half or front so that the cat can see out, but some nervous cats prefer not to see out. Cats feel very safe in a carrier—the confinement is reassuring—and using a

carrier is by far the easiest way to transport the cat
to the veterinarian, groomer, or boarding kennel.
Carriers come in a variety of styles and materials
and are available from any pet supply store.

You, Your Cat, And The Veterinarian

As soon as you acquire a cat, you should have it
checked out by a veterinarian. If you've never
owned a cat before, how do you locate a good
veterinarian? First, ask your pet-owning friends—
they're probably as familiar with their veterinarian
as with their physician and chose him or her for
the same reasons: professional competence, reasonable fees, convenience of hours and location, and
genuine interest in his or her patients. If none of
your friends are pet owners, call up the local veterinary association and ask for recommendations; they
may not give you a single name, but you can be
sure that the names they do give you will be those
of practitioners they consider to be reputable.

Once you've decided on a veterinarian, call up,
introduce yourself, and arrange to visit the facility.
Veterinarians are often very busy, but they are
always happy to show you around.

What are you looking for in this initial visit to
the veterinarian? Basically, you're checking out
these points:

• Is the facility clean, orderly, and pleasant? A
veterinarian's office should be as clean as your own
doctor's office.

31

• Is emergency service available? If your cat gets sick or is involved in an accident out of office hours, what will you do? Many veterinarians belong to emergency clinics that function after their own hospital closes. Be sure that your veterinarian is a member of such a clinic, or has some other adequate emergency service available.

• Is the veterinarian willing to answer all your questions? A good veterinarian will be able to answer your questions in understandable terms—you and the veterinarian, after all, are partners in caring for your pet's health. Your vet should also explain the fee scale for different services.

• Are the two of you going to get along on a professional level? It's important that you feel comfortable with the person who'll be caring for your pet. Lack of communication is one of the most common reasons that client and veterinarian part company.

If, during your initial visit, either the facility or the veterinarian fails to impress you, go elsewhere.

Communication between client and veterinarian works both ways. Treat the veterinarian as you would your own doctor. Don't make unnecessary calls at inconvenient times. Do your own part to maintain your cat's health through proper nutrition and regular checkups. Follow the veterinarian's instructions precisely. And, as you become a more experienced cat owner, use your judgment to decide what is an emergency and what isn't.

Your cat's first visit to the veterinarian's office should be within a few days of the new pet's arrival in your home. At this first visit, your veterinarian will give the cat a thorough physical examination, and, if the cat is a kitten, administer the first of the series of vaccinations that are necessary to protect the animal against a number of feline diseases. At this time, the veterinarian will also advise on diet and set up a future vaccination schedule for the cat. (Further information on vaccinations is given in a later chapter.) If your cat is a kitten, this first visit to the veterinarian should take place between the ages of six and eight weeks. The veterinarian will need to see the kitten several more times during the next few months.

Remember to take a sample of the cat's stool along to the veterinarian's office. The stool will be analyzed for parasites and, if necessary, a worming schedule will be set up.

Elective Surgery

Your initial visit to the veterinarian is an appropriate time to discuss having the cat neutered. Apart from the obvious advantage of avoiding accidental parenthood—an inevitability in the case of an unneutered cat that's allowed outside—both male and female animals can benefit from neutering. The procedure reduces the incidence of certain health problems, and, contrary to what you may have heard, neutering does not have adverse effects on the cat's personality.

Neutering comes under the heading of "elective surgery"—surgery that you choose to have done even though it is not necessitated by any direct health problem.

The Female Cat And The Facts Of Life

The female cat reaches sexual maturity some-where between five and eight months of age. The cat's heat season occurs twice a year and in each season she may cycle in and out of heat two or three times. Thus, the female cat can be in heat as many as six times a year.

A female cat is made incapable of breeding by a surgical procedure called ovariohysterectomy, more commonly known as spaying. This involves the removal of the ovaries and the uterus; the female's heat periods stop and she cannot, of course, have kittens.

Ideally, the female cat should be spayed at about six months of age, before the heat cycles normally begin, when the procedure is simpler and recovery is faster. However, spaying can be done at any age with no lasting ill effects. Spaying while she's young significantly reduces the cat's risk of breast cancer and prevents infection of the uterus (pyo-metra). Spaying also stops her from trying to es-cape from the house each time you open the door. And, most important from the point of view of your own convenience, the cessation of the heat cycle means you won't have a mob of very vocal feline suitors around your home up to six times a year.

Spaying does alter the metabolism of the female cat to some extent, and she may put on weight unless her diet is controlled.

Spaying is done under a general anesthetic. An incision is made in the abdomen, the ovaries and uterus are removed, and the incision is closed with stitches. The cat must be kept quiet for three to four days, and the stitches can usually be removed after 10 days.

The Male Cat And The Facts Of Life

The male usually becomes sexually mature at 11 to 12 months of age, and in most cases the signs will be all too evident to the owner. The cat may begin to spray urine around the house, back up against furniture or drapes with its tail held high and quivering, and urinate in a standing position. This behavior is a way of marking its territory. The strong male odor of the urine is supposed to invite all female cats into his territory and warn other males that it "owns" the area. The male cat's desire to roam increases; he may be reluctant to stay in the house, and he's likely to vocalize at odd hours—usually while you are sleeping.

Neutering, or castrating, the male cat involves the surgical removal of both testes from the scrotum. It is a simple, inexpensive procedure and presents few problems. It's done in the veterinary hospital under general anesthetic and the cat can usually go home the same or the next day. Most veterinarians advise that the male cat should be neutered at the age of eight to nine months.

Neutering usually reduces or eliminates the above-mentioned bad habits without altering the cat's basic personality—he may even become more affectionate. It's not true that neutered cats become fat and lazy. However, weight gain after neutering is possible if the cat is overfed, so diet control is important.

A big advantage of neutering is that it lessens the cat's chances of getting into fights with other tomcats. These fights between males inflict a lot of bites that develop into painful abscesses.

Declawing

Declawing is a surgical procedure that involves removing the nails from their attachment to the toes. It's done to stop the cat from wrecking the furniture by scratching it. The surgery is performed under general anesthesia and requires a couple days of hospitalization. The stitches usually dissolve by themselves. Declawing is a service to the owner, not to the cat. However, despite the many horror stories you may have heard about declawing (none of them are true), declawed cats live a normal life, jump as high as they used to, run, and hide from danger, just as they did when they had claws. They do not become biters to compensate for no longer having claws.

If you get a cat as a kitten, you may (as mentioned earlier) be able to avoid having it declawed by training it early to sharpen its claws on a scratching post instead of on your antique tapestry loveseat. Despite all efforts, however, some cats spurn a scratching post and continue to tear up the furniture. In the effort to continue to make that cat a welcome pet, you may decide to have it declawed. Most veterinarians recommend declawing only the front two paws; the back ones seldom inflict damage to you or the furniture. If you are in doubt, discuss the procedure with your veterinarian. After a cat is declawed, the cat's feet will be tender for up to a week. The veterinarian may also advise you to use shredded newspaper instead of litter in the box for a few days to lessen the chances of irritation and infection.

Saying Goodbye

Hard as it may be to think of—especially when you've just acquired a healthy, young cat—one of the services your veterinarian may one day have to perform for you is euthanizing your pet. Cats age faster than people and begin to fail much earlier. Often an aging cat will lose a lot of weight, want to sleep all day, or become disoriented. Some older cats start to urinate and defecate in the house. Old age may also bring loss of sight or hearing. Watching an animal you love become debilitated through age or through chronic disease is one of the saddest parts of owning and caring for it.

How do you make that all too final decision to end the cat's life? When your pet can no longer function as a pet or lead a full, comfortable existence, then it's time to make the decision to euthanize it.

All pet owners, of course, hope that the decision may never have to be made—that one day they'll wake up to find that their elderly or sick cat has died in its sleep. Unfortunately, it seldom happens that way, and unless the owner makes the decision to spare the cat any more suffering, it may die a miserable or agonizing death. Although it's hard at the time, the decision to euthanize a cat that's either too old or too sick to go on living content-edly is one you cannot regret.

When the question arises, you should discuss it with all family members, including the children, and then with your veterinarian. In fact, the veterinarian is often the first one to realize and suggest the need to put the cat to sleep.

Euthanasia is a painless procedure in which a drug is injected into the cat. The drug simply acts first to put the cat to sleep, and then to stop the heart. You may want to be with your cat while it's done, but sometimes it's wiser to remember it as it used to be and to let the veterinarian perform the euthanasia alone.

Whichever decision is made, all members of the family must be aware of what is happening. It's particularly important that children understand that the procedure is the best thing for the cat and that it won't hurt it.

Grieving

The loss of a pet causes its owner to feel the same grief feelings as if a member of the family had died. Often it is difficult for a pet owner to express his or her feelings because it is often socially unacceptable to do so. Non-pet owners don't understand the attachment that developed and sometimes belittle the strong feelings felt by the pet owner. Consequently, expressing grief externally is often not done, but it should be expressed.

The stages of grief for loss of a pet are identical to the stages for loss of a human loved one:

Denial. This is the first stage and involves the owner not admitting that his or her pet is dying or has died. This is a difficult stage to deal with since psychologists believe that denial occurs at the subconscious level.

Bargaining. In this stage, the pet owner, when faced with a terminally ill pet, promises never to discipline the pet again and will offer it the best food available, if only it will get better.

Anger. Anger is exhibited either at others or at oneself. The hostility exhibited to others, including the veterinarian, must be recognized for what it is. Self anger is manifested as guilt and is one of the most common cases of grieving. The pet owner feels he or she did something wrong to cause the pet to die or be sick.

Grief. This stage is the sad stage of grieving. This stage can lead to depression and altering of one's day-to-day activities. Psychologists agree that this is the stage that needs the most support. Grieving pet owners need to talk to someone about their feelings. If the feelings persist for a long time, or the pet owner feels severe depression, professional assistance may be necessary. Help can be obtained by contacting your veterinarian for guidance.

Resolution. This is the final stage of grieving. Since it is the acceptance stage of death, the pet owner is often ready to accept a new pet or at least give thought to the idea.

Pet Insurance

Medical care of pets is becoming very sophisticated. Cats are living longer today than ever before thanks to medical advances that involve disease prevention and cure. Consequently, the costs of care have risen and it is not unusual for a cat with cancer to incur hundreds of dollars in medical costs to place it into remission. As a result, pet insurance companies have appeared on the scene. The cost of pet insurance is very reasonable, and although the insurance companies don't pay for everything, they pick up a large portion of the costs of most serious illnesses.

NUTRITION: HOW TO KEEP YOUR CAT WELL-FED

In their natural state, cats are basically carnivores—meat-eating animals. In the wild, the cat catches its prey (mice, rats, birds, and so on) and eats the whole animal, including the internal organs, bone, skin, muscle, and whatever material is in the intestines and stomach of the prey. By devouring the whole prey in this manner, the cat gets a nutritionally balanced meal.

Since the cat became a domestic animal, scientists have studied its nutritional needs and have come up with very specific requirements. And what the owner regards as a "natural" all-meat diet does not meet those requirements. The large number of commercial cat foods available today are of excellent nutritional quality and reflect the findings of a great deal of research by the manufacturers. A cat can get a perfectly satisfactory and healthy diet from commercially available products.

The single worst thing you can do as a cat owner, however, is to feed the cat a diet of table-food scraps that cannot meet a cat's rigid nutritional requirements, and there are other "don'ts" that are equally important. Contrary to popular belief, cats should not be fed milk—it's a poor food source, and it often causes diarrhea. An all-meat or all-fish diet will certainly result in severe deficiencies and probably either cause disease or make the cat more susceptible to it.

Unlike dogs, who will eat the same thing day after day without complaint, cats are not monotonous eaters. Most cats enjoy a variety of flavors and textures. Some cats won't complain if you serve the same food daily, but others demand frequent changes of menu. The different types of cat foods available enable you to satisfy a gourmet cat's taste for a varied diet.

Commercial cat food comes in three basic forms— dry, semi-moist, and canned—and these are described below.

Dry cat foods. These are so named because they contain only seven to 12 percent moisture. Most brands contain about 30 percent protein and eight to 10 percent fat. All the different brands have basically the same content of vitamins, essential amino acids, and minerals in proportions specifically dictated by the cat's requirements. Most dry foods supply approximately 1600 to 1700 calories per pound of product. *Note:* A cat should never be fed dry dog food on a regular basis; the cat needs more protein and fat than a dog, and the two animals should be fed only the commercial foods formulated to meet the dietary needs of their own species.

Semi-moist (soft-moist) foods. These contain about 30 percent moisture and usually come in sealed one- or two-meal packages. Semi-moist cat foods normally contain about 24 percent protein and 10 percent fat and supply about 1500 calories per pound of product.

Canned cat foods. Canned foods have a high moisture content—approximately 70 to 80 percent—and vary in protein content. They provide 500 to 600 calories per pound of product. "Specialty" canned foods contain 10 to 12 percent protein and appeal to the cat who needs a variety of flavors and tastes. However, some of these are all-meat products and do not provide a balanced diet. They should be fed only with the addition of a complete food such as one of the dry or semi-moist products discussed earlier. Some canned foods have a protein content as high as 23 percent; nevertheless, look at the label to check if the food will provide a 100 percent balanced diet. If so, the label will say "100 percent complete" or "nutritionally complete and balanced."

The amount of food that your cat or kitten requires each day depends on many factors, of which activity, age, environment, and sex are just a few. Indoor cats, for instance, always eat less than outdoor cats. Since no two cats will eat the same amount of food, it will be necessary for you to experiment to see how much your particular cat needs. Cats won't usually eat food just because it's there, or eat when they're no longer hungry. There are exceptions, however, and as a rule it's not recommended to leave food down all day. Once your cat gets in the habit of overeating, it'll start to put on weight, and obesity in cats—as in people—is difficult to reverse.

The nutrition charts on pages 45 and 47 give an approximation of how much food a healthy cat needs at different stages of development. Quantities are given according to body weight. Note that these amounts apply only to healthy cats living in a normal domestic environment. Sick or debilitated cats, some kittens, and pregnant females all have specific dietary requirements and should be fed according to the recommendations of a vet.

In order to use these charts, you must know how many calories there are per cup, package, or can of product you are feeding. This information should be available on the food package or from the manufacturer. As a guide:

1 cup of dry food = 290 calories
1 pkg. semi-moist food (1½ oz) = 125 calories
1 can food (6½ oz) = 250 calories

To use the kitten chart, find your cat's age in the top line and its weight in the left-hand column. The figure where the two intersect gives you the cat's calorie requirements at that age. For instance, at 16 weeks old, a 4 lb. kitten needs 320 calories a day. Note that the kitten's daily needs decrease as it gets older.

Feeding A Kitten

When you take an eight-week-old kitten home, it should be completely weaned. Kittens usually nurse until they're five to six weeks old, although when left to themselves (and provided that their mother is cooperative) they may continue to nurse until they're nine or 10 weeks old. Weaning (giving solid food) should start when the kitten is four to five weeks old; by six to eight weeks it's well able to handle regular food.

When you bring your kitten home, start it on a regular feeding schedule right away; this means feeding at the same times each day. In the first days, stay with the type of food the kitten was weaned on—canned, semi-moist, or dry. If you're using dry food, moisten it with a little water. A good steady diet is dry food with a complete canned food mixed in as a supplement. Feed the kitten three or four times a day; by the time it's six months old, it will need to be fed only twice a day.

DAILY CALORIE REQUIREMENTS FOR KITTENS

Weight		Age					
		6 weeks	3 months	4 months	6 months	8 months	1 year
kgs.	lbs.	Calories Per Day					
.45	1	110	90	80	55	40	30
.91	2	220	180	160	110	80	60
1.4	3	330	270	240	165	120	90
1.8	4		360	320	220	160	120
2.3	5			400	275	200	150
2.7	6			480	330	240	180
3.2	7				385	280	210
3.6	8				440	320	240
4.1	9				495	360	270
4.5	10					400	300

- These figures are based on the results of scientific studies on cat nutrition.
- Note that a kitten's daily calorie needs decrease as it gets older.

The way you train your kitten will set its pattern for the way it eats as an adult, so establish good eating habits right away. Leave the food dish down for no longer than 10 to 15 minutes. When the kitten walks away, assume it's had enough and pick the food up. If it gobbles up the food and looks around for more, give it some more. If the kitten walks away from the dish without eating, don't assume that it doesn't like the cuisine and offer it something else. Remember that you're the provider and you set the schedule. If it rejects the food when you put it down, remove it until the next meal. Don't give in if it looks hungry 10 minutes later, and don't offer it table food; this will just establish lifelong bad habits and let it know that it can manipulate you to feed it on demand.

Many cat owners leave food down for the cat all day on the assumption that cats are "nibblers" who like to eat little and often, and that cats don't eat when they're not hungry. This is certainly true of many cats, but there are exceptions. By establishing regular feeding times, you remove the temptation to overeat and avoid the inevitable result of over-eating—a fat cat.

Leave fresh water down for the cat at all times, although cats are not big water drinkers; many cats get most of their water from licking at a dripping faucet. A cat on a canned-food diet will get most of its water supply from its food.

Feeding The Adult Cat

An adult cat should be fed twice per day, prefer-ably—since cats are creatures of habit—at the same

DAILY CALORIE REQUIREMENTS FOR ADULT CATS

Weight kgs.	lbs.	Calories Per Day
2.3	5	150
2.7	6	180
3.2	7	210
3.6	8	240
4.1	9	270
4.5	10	300
5.0	11	330
5.5	12	360

• These figures are based on the results of scientific studies on cat nutrition.

times and in the same place every time. Remember that table food can be detrimental to your cat's health, so never allow the cat up on any surface that has food on it (cats are very adept at helping themselves from the dinner table or kitchen counter when your back is turned).

If you're giving your adult cat canned food, give it one small can (6½ oz) each day. If you're adding dry food, give half a cup and reduce the canned food accordingly. If you're giving dry food alone, one (8 oz) cup per day is sufficient. If semi-moist food is fed, the cat should not require more than one to two half-ounce packages each day. Remember that these amounts apply only to a normal, healthy, five- to 10-pound cat and are only estimates. Remember also that it is better to underfeed than to overfeed, and that a cat should never be fed cold food, table scraps, raw fish, or any type of raw meat.

It's okay to add boiled chicken or liver to the cat's food as long as this is only an occasional treat. However, you should never let such special treats

TOXIC PLANTS

Algerian Ivy	Daffodil	Marijuana
Amaryllis	Dieffenbachia	Mistletoe
Arrowhead Vine	(dumbcane,	Philodendron
Asparagus Fern	mother–in–law	(heart leaf)
Avocado	plant)	Poppy
Azalea	Dracaena Palm	Pothos
Bird of Paradise	Elephant Ears	(devil's ivy)
Boston Ivy	English Holly	Schefflera
Caladium	English Ivy	Snow–on–the
Calla Lily	Hydrangea	Mountain
Castor Bean	Iris	Spathiphyllum
Christmas Rose	Japanese Yew	Spider Plant
Chrysanthemum	Jerusalem	Tulip
Corn Plant	Cherry	Weeping Fig
Crown of	Lily of the	(ficus)
Thorns	Valley	

become a major portion of the cat's diet.

If you have a cat that's particularly partial to nibbling on your houseplants (an annoyance to you and a real danger to the cat), grow some grass or parsley indoors for the cat to chew on instead. The cat may still prefer the houseplants, in which case you will have to protect or remove the plants.

Always remember that feeding bones to cats is asking for trouble. Since commercial cat food contains all the minerals the cat needs, bones are not necessary and can be a serious hazard, causing intestinal obstruction, constipation, or perforation of the bowel.

Feeding The Older Cat

As the cat ages, all its functions slow down. It sleeps more and gets much less exercise, and often it will reduce its food intake. Occasionally, an older cat will eat voraciously but still appear to lose weight. Weight loss is not unusual in older cats but the veterinarian should see the older cat regularly—at least every year—to assess its general health. It's best to have your veterinarian advise you on an appropriate diet for your older cat based on the animal's health. You should also be certain to report immediately any abnormality or change in the cat's food or water intake.

Special Diets

There are many health conditions in cats that require the animal to be put on a special diet. A cat with kidney disease, for example, needs a diet containing a high-quality protein in low quantity. Disorders such as heart disease, liver disease, and intestinal or stomach problems all require dietary adaptations.

It's possible to cook at home a diet that will meet the requirements of the problem being treated, but it is far easier to buy a commercially prepared diet food from your veterinarian. These foods are palatable (to the cat) and easy to use (for your convenience) and they contain the required balance of vitamins and minerals. These special foods cost a bit more than regular commercial cat foods because only high-quality materials are used, and they're only available through the vet.

THE SOCIAL CAT: TRAINING AND TRAVEL

The cat is a very independent animal, and many cat owners will tell you that it is this independence that makes the cat such a comfortable companion around the house. Cats are not as demanding of attention as dogs. And, unlike dogs, most cats don't make any particular effort to win your approval—they'll often wait for you to come to them rather than run around trying to catch your eye, and their ways of expressing affection are less obtrusive than those of dogs.

All this means that the cat is a very easygoing creature, polite, and self-possessed. But it also means that it's difficult to train a cat. If you and the cat don't see eye to eye over a certain kind of behavior, you're probably going to have a hard time getting it to do things your way.

Getting A Cat To Change Its Ways

Training a cat to use a litter pan (as discussed in the chapter, "Your Cat Becomes One Of The Family") is usually a straightforward matter. The cat is naturally clean, and a litter pan duplicates the soil where it would eliminate and cover up its urine and feces outdoors.

There are times, however, when you need to train the cat not to do something that annoys you—like jumping on the kitchen counter or sleeping on top of the papers on your desk. Unlike the dog, who will change its behavior in order to please you and earn your approval, a cat prefers to please itself. So verbal discipline doesn't usually work with a cat. You can try it, however. When you see the cat jumping on the counter, say "no" firmly and follow up with a loud noise that will startle the cat—shaking an empty can filled with dried beans makes a satisfactory clatter.

If this doesn't work—and it often won't—get a squirt gun or plant mister and keep it handy. Every time the cat does something objectionable or comes near a forbidden place or object, spray it in the face with the water. It will hate this, and if you do it regularly you should soon get to the point where just the presence of the squirt gun or mister will deter it from the objectionable behavior.

Don't ever use physical discipline on a cat. It may relieve your temper, but it will do nothing to prevent the cat from repeating whatever bad behavior provoked the discipline. You may also end up with a scared cat who cringes away from your hand. So if a stern voice doesn't work, stick with the squirt gun.

There are situations, of course, where passive resistance is the best course, and some of these are discussed elsewhere in this book. For instance, a cat that habitually sharpens its claws on the sofa can—if it's introduced to it young enough—be persuaded to use a scratching post instead. If not, you can discuss with the veterinarian the procedure of removing the cat's front claws (see the section on elective surgery). And if your cat persists in eating your houseplants (annoying for you and dangerous for it) and can't be distracted by a pot of parsley, grass, or catnip for its own use, either move the plants out of reach or hang them from the ceiling.

Coping With An Aggressive Cat

Although domestic cats are generally social creatures, they retain the instincts they had in the wild. In their natural state, cats hunt and attack prey, and even a cat living with humans who provide good food may exhibit aggressive behavior.

Kittens express their aggressive instincts in play. They love to stalk and attack your hands and feet. In a little kitten, this can be cute (although kittens have teeth and nails like needles), but it's a mistake to let the kitten grow up thinking that it's okay to play rough. As mentioned earlier, physical discipline is never appropriate. You can, however, train the kitten to direct its attacking behavior to something other than your toes. When it starts to play rough, distract it with a favorite toy or a ball attached to a piece of string or yarn. Do this consistently and it will usually learn to displace the attack to the toy.

If the kitten still prefers to fight your feet, or if you've got an older cat that's used to playing rough, you may need to use the squirt gun or spray mister mentioned earlier. Still offer the toy, and if the cat attacks the toy instead of you, praise it a lot. If it attacks you, spray it in the face with water.

If it's particularly reluctant to play your way, add a little cider vinegar to the water to make it particularly distasteful to the cat. Tell it "no" loudly at the same time that you spray. Consistent discipline of this kind will usually get satisfactory results.

Dealing with an aggressive adult cat is different from teaching a kitten good manners. If a normally good-natured cat suddenly becomes aggressive, there's always an explanation. Either its attacking behavior has never been disciplined, or it's reacting to some stressful situation that's bringing out its instinctive aggression. A cat that's sick will become aggressive, and it's always wise to have the veterinarian check out any cat that's showing a change in behavior so that illness can be either identified or ruled out.

If the cat is not sick, you need to examine the environment for stressful situations such as loud noise, family fights, or rough handling. Any such situation may cause a normally even-tempered cat to become aggressive, and removing the cause of the stress should restore its usual good temper.

If you get a grown cat from a shelter, you should try to check out its past and get the shelter staff's comments on its temperament. A cat that has been mishandled in the past may be aggressive or become aggressive under stress. There's seldom much you can do about this, so if you're getting a cat for the family it's best not to choose one that has had a difficult past. Such a cat needs a quiet, relaxed home and, although it couldn't cope with a houseful of kids, it would probably make a fine pet for someone living alone.

Traveling With Your Cat

Cats can be very good travelers, especially if they become accustomed to traveling while they're young. Unfortunately, the most common journeys you make with your cat are probably to the veterinarian or the grooming establishment, both anxiety-producing trips that are likely to make your cat expect nothing but trouble any time it's put in the car.

You can avoid this negative attitude to travel by putting the cat in its carrier and doing a few trial runs before you actually go anywhere else. (Remember, though, that your traveling cat must always wear an I.D. tag.) Using a cat carrier, which is described in the chapter, "Your Cat Becomes One Of The Family," is the perfect way to transport the cat. It can't get under your feet, under the seat, or out of the car. And the confinement of the carrier is comforting to the cat.

The only time you need to take the cat out of the carrier while traveling is to let it use the litter box on an exceptionally long trip. If the carrier is large enough, you can put a small pan of litter inside the carrier. Otherwise, keep a litter pan in the trunk of the car and, when you stop to let the cat use it, put a harness and leash on it before you open the car door. Be very careful to do this, because if the cat panics and jumps from the car in a strange place, it'll surely get lost.

Do not feed the cat before a car journey. If it has the least tendency to get car-sick, food will certainly make it vomit on the trip. If you're in the car for more than four or five hours, give it a little water. Be sure to call any hotel or motel you plan to stop at to make sure they accept pets.

Don't ever leave the cat unattended in a closed car on a hot day. The most common cause of heat prostration and subsequent death in cats is over-heating in a hot automobile. If you must leave the cat (or any other animal) in the car, park the car in the shade and leave the windows partially open. However, don't leave the cat unless it's absolutely necessary. An excited or nervous cat in a closed, hot car can overheat in a matter of minutes, and brain damage follows very quickly.

Checking Travel Regulations

Specific regulations apply to cats traveling by air or on other forms of public transportation, and you should always check them out before a trip. Air-lines require that the cat be enclosed in a carrier or crate. If the carrier is small enough to go under your seat in the aircraft, the cat can travel with you; otherwise, the animal must travel in the bag-gage compartment. The baggage compartment is pressurized and the temperature controlled, so your cat would come to no harm (beyond, proba-bly, being lonely and somewhat apprehensive). However, most airlines sell carriers that will fit neatly under your seat. Attach identification to the crate, along with copies of any health certification required by the state or foreign country to which the cat is traveling.

If you're traveling to a foreign country, contact the consulate for that country and have them send you the forms you and your vet have to complete before taking an animal into the country. Frequently, your state Department of Agriculture will have to approve the documents—so don't leave those arrangements until the last minute.

Wherever you're traveling, take your cat to the veterinarian at least two weeks before your departure date. The veterinarian will make sure all the cat's vaccinations are up to date and review the cat's medical condition. Whether you are flying or driving, your veterinarian may consider it necessary to prescribe a tranquilizer to calm the cat and prevent motion sickness.

The Stay-At-Home Cat

Many times it may not be possible to travel with your cat—or your cat may not like to travel. There are many reputable boarding establishments where you can board your cat while you're away. However, it will be much less traumatic for the cat if it can stay home and you can arrange for a neighbor or a pet-sitting service to come in daily to give it food and water and check that it's well.

If you decide to board your cat, ask your veterinarian if he or she has boarding facilities—some do. Otherwise, get recommendations from your friends or the veterinarian and, if possible, visit several boarding establishments before you make your choice. Look for cleanliness and a caring staff, and don't patronize any operator that seems reluctant to have you tour the facility; reputable establishments are always happy to show you around. The American Boarding Kennels Association (ABKA) makes available a list of member establishments along with advice on how to select a boarding establishment. You can write to the ABKA at 4575 Galley Road #400A, Colorado Springs, CO 80915. Once you've decided where to board your cat, make the reservation as early as possible. Good establishments fill up fast at vacation time.

Before you leave your pet in the charge of anyone—friend or professional—make sure the person is fully aware of the animal's feeding schedule, habits, fears, idiosyncrasies, and so on. Make sure the cat's vaccinations are current, and leave the phone numbers of your veterinarian and his or her emergency service. Then you can enjoy your trip, confident in the knowledge that your cat will be well cared for in your absence.

GROOMING: THE GOOD-LOOKING CAT

Good grooming is as important to your cat as it is to you. A well-groomed cat looks good and feels good, and grooming sessions serve two useful purposes beyond the obvious goal of cleanliness: They are (or should be) fun for you both, and they give you a chance to do a quick check on your cat's general health. While it is true that cats—or most cats—groom themselves regularly and are very fastidious about keeping themselves clean, extra grooming enhances the cat's appearance and helps remove dead hair. This is important, especially in the case of a long-haired cat, because the hair a cat swallows during grooming can form hairballs in the cat's stomach.

Grooming involves caring not only for the cat's coat, but also for the eyes, ears, nails, and mouth. The amount of grooming your cat needs depends a lot on whether it's a short-haired or long-haired type, and you'll have taken this into account before you took the cat into your home.

Combing and brushing are the first steps to keeping your cat well-groomed. Combing separates the tangled hair at skin level; brushing removes dead hair and gives luster to the coat. Long-haired cats like Persians and Ragdolls need to be combed and brushed twice a day to prevent the hair from

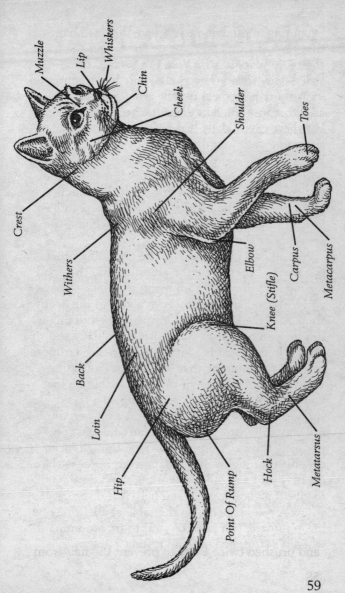

Muzzle
Lip
Whiskers
Chin
Cheek
Shoulder
Toes
Crest
Withers
Elbow
Knee (Stifle)
Carpus
Metacarpus
Back
Loin
Hip
Point Of Rump
Hock
Metatarsus

becoming matted and to remove the dead hair so that the cat won't swallow it. The longer the hair, the more work it is for you, but each of these twice-daily sessions need take only five minutes or so. A short-haired cat usually won't need combing at all because the hair doesn't often tangle or mat. For these cats, a daily brushing is adequate. When grooming your long-haired cat, comb through the hair, then brush the hair in the direction of growth with a medium-stiff brush. Just before the end of the grooming session, brush against the direction of growth so that the bristles reach the deep under-layers of hair. Always brush the stomach and the areas under the legs.

Not all cats take kindly to the grooming process, but most of them love the attention and the good feeling that they get from being groomed—just as you feel good after a shower or a visit to the beauty shop. And the best way to insure that grooming is fun for you both is to start with short, daily sessions when the cat is a kitten—kittens are far more tolerant of grooming than adult cats. The easiest way to groom a kitten or cat is on a table, so that you won't have to stoop. Just being on a raised surface will probably make the cat a bit nervous, so it'll stay still instead of moving around and complicating things. A slippery surface, though, may upset it thoroughly and is dangerous because the cat may skid and fall. Put a rubber mat on the table to give it a good footing and help it feel secure. If your cat resents being on the table at all, it may be less traumatic (for both of you) to try grooming it when it's stretched out and resting.

Make the first grooming sessions short—just a few minutes a day—and heap your cat with praise at the end of each successful session. Tell it how proud you are of it and how beautiful it looks. Pretty soon it'll be looking forward to grooming sessions and the attention that accompanies them. Don't give up if your early attempts to groom your kitten are frustrating. Take it slowly, and be generous with your praise. Soon you'll probably have it purring contentedly at grooming time.

As your cat gets used to being groomed, make sure that you handle all parts of its body during the process. Look at its eyes and ears; open its mouth and run your fingers along its gums. This way the cat will get used to your touch and you'll have a much easier job when the time comes to give it medication or inspect or clean its teeth.

If The Cat Won't Cooperate

If you happen to have a cat that—despite all your care and approval—hates to be touched, you'll have to use different tactics. You may need to recruit another family member to hold the cat while you groom it. If it's a long-haired cat with hair that mats easily, and if you just can't handle it without getting scratched to bits, ask your veterinarian to recommend a grooming establishment. The short-haired cat that's difficult to handle and won't let you groom it can probably be left to take care of its own grooming.

One of the abiding disadvantages of owning a cat is shedding. Shedding is controlled by the amount of light in the cat's environment. If your cat is exposed to natural daylight only, it will probably shed only twice a year. However, indoor cats are exposed to artificial light and shed frequently, sometimes heavily. While a certain amount of shedding (maybe more than you're happy with) is normal, excessive shedding should be brought to the attention of your veterinarian.

What Grooming Equipment Will You Need?

The equipment you need to keep your cat looking good is very basic. These are the essentials:

Brush and comb. If you've got a short-haired cat, use a medium-stiff brush to keep its coat in shape. It'll find it very comforting, too, provided you remember always to brush in the direction of the

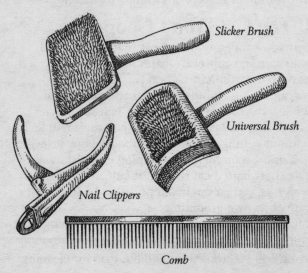

Slicker Brush

Universal Brush

Nail Clippers

Comb

hair. With a long-haired cat, you'll need to use first a comb to separate the tangled hair, then a medium-stiff brush.

It's important to choose the right brush, and the best kind for all-around use is a soft-wire slicker brush, which is between the very soft brushes used on show cats and the harsh slicker brushes sold in many pet stores. Natural bristle brushes are good but don't remove the dead hair nearly as effectively as the slicker brush. If the cat's coat is badly matted, a Universal brush (like a slicker brush but convex in shape) removes the mats much better than a slicker brush. When you're buying a comb, choose one that has half fine and half coarse teeth. The illustration on page 62 shows some of the grooming aids available in pet supply stores.

Nail clippers. Most cats tend to sharpen their claws on the furniture. If you have not had your cat declawed (see the section on elective surgery), clipping the nails can save you a lot of furniture repair bills. Don't ever use human nail clippers on your cat. You can get special cat nail clippers from any pet supply store. If you don't know what to get, ask your vet for a recommendation.

Shampoo. You can buy pet shampoo at a pet supply store—not just from a veterinarian. Human shampoos are very drying and not recommended for your pet.

Miscellaneous Supplies. Your grooming kit can usefully include a number of other items, many of which you may already have in your home: mineral oil (a drop in each eye before bathing prevents eye irritations); cotton swabs and baby oil for cleaning the ears; cotton balls and a commercial eyewash to use in the case of simple eye irritations; a child's toothbrush or cotton balls to clean the teeth; and styptic powder for use on a bleeding nail.

Bathing A Cat

Why bathe a cat? Cats get dirty just like dogs, especially if they go outside. And if they pick up fleas, a flea bath is certainly in order. Since not all cats take to water easily (a lot of them hate it), you can try bathing your cat with plain water to see how it reacts. If it puts up a terrible fuss, you're likely to get bitten or clawed so you might as well give up the whole idea. If the reluctant cat is exceptionally dirty, or has managed to get road tar or car grease on its coat, you will have to have it professionally groomed.

A drop of mineral oil in each eye prevents irritation from soap at bathtime.

If, however, your cat takes well to the water and bathing it seems like a reasonable proposition, the best place to do it is in a sink or basin. Before bathing, use a dropper to place one drop of mineral oil into each of the cat's eyes (see illustration); this will protect the eyes from the shampoo. Fill the sink with warm water to reach the cat's elbows, and lower it carefully into the water. Then shampoo it, talking encouragingly to it in a soothing voice. Do not submerge the cat or frighten it by splashing the water around, and keep the shampoo out of its eyes. After lathering the cat, rinse it well. If you're bathing it in the kitchen sink and you have a spray attachment on the faucet, use the spray to rinse it. Otherwise, empty the sink and fill it with fresh water. Towel-dry the cat thoroughly and keep it indoors until it's completely dry.

Some cats will tolerate having their hair blown dry with a hair dryer—on low heat only. But test the cat's reaction to the blow dryer before actually using it on the cat—the noise may frighten it. One useful strategy is to place the cat in the cat carrier that you use for trips to the veterinarian, and let the hair dryer blow through the wire front or sides of the carrier. Even though the noise of the dryer would normally frighten the cat, it feels secure within the confined space of the carrier. After it is dry, brush the fur thoroughly to remove loose and dead hair.

When you're bathing or grooming your cat, you have the ideal opportunity for checking out the skin all over the body for any irritations or lesions that may need attention. At this time, check also for fleas and ticks. If you find them, deal with them as discussed in the chapter on parasites.

General Care At Grooming Time

Whether you're bathing your cat or just brushing and combing it, part of the grooming session should include attention to the eyes, ears, nails, and teeth.

A healthy cat's eyes should always be bright and shining, with wide-open lids. When you're grooming the cat, use a cotton ball dipped in warm water to gently wipe away any discharge that has accumulated in the corners of the eyes; any time there's a green or yellow discharge from the eyes, you should call the veterinarian. This is particularly important if the discharge is accompanied by redness of the eyes.

Another cause for veterinary attention is excessive tearing; the veterinarian will check that the tear ducts are functioning properly. Persians frequently tear a lot and develop brown stains on the fur between the corners of the eyes and the mouth. Provided that the veterinarian has determined that the tearing is normal, there's nothing you can do about the discoloration. Chronic tearing is also common in cats that have had upper respiratory viruses when young.

Clean your cat's ears routinely, once a week. Cleaning the ears is a relatively easy task provided that you take a few simple precautions. You may require an assistant to hold the cat for you, and you should use cotton-tipped swabs dipped in baby oil—never use alcohol or any other solvent.

The ear canal is "L" shaped, going straight down and then turning in toward the head; at the end of the "L" is the eardrum. To clean the ear, hold the ear flap (or pinna) straight up above the head and gently place the cotton-tipped swab into the canal in a vertical position; that is, facing down toward the floor. This way the swab cannot enter far enough into the canal to harm the eardrum. Using a very gentle rotating motion, clean out the wax and debris from the ear folds and crevices. If there's heavy brown debris in the ears, an unpleasant odor from the ears, or if the cat scratches at the ear or tilts its head persistently to one side, call the veterinarian.

Cats' nails are sharp and curved, and cats seem to spend a lot of time keeping them extra sharp. Outside cats generally wear down their nails in the course of normal activities, but an indoor cat's nails are usually as sharp as razor blades. If the nails become too long, they can get caught in the carpet or upholstery and they frequently break off, so an indoor cat should have its claws clipped once a month—or more frequently if necessary. Never use human clippers on the cat's nails. Special clippers are available from any pet supply store, and if you are in doubt about what kind to get, ask your veterinarian for a recommendation.

You may need someone to hold the cat while you clip the nails, and before you start to cut, you should examine the nails to make sure you know what you're doing. Each nail has a blood vessel and a nerve—the quick. If you cut into the quick, you'll hurt the cat and make the nail bleed. If the cat has white or pale nails (most cats do), you can see the quick as a pink line running in the nail.

Exposing the cat's nails can be a tricky maneuver. Place the paw in your hand and place your thumb on top of the paw, close to the nails, with your index finger on the large pad on the bottom of the paw. Press your thumb and finger together. This will expose the nails for clipping. Using the

The correct way to clip a cat's nails

special cat nail clippers described earlier, cut the nail a little below the quick (just in front of the pink blood vessel). When you are clipping the nails, don't forget to clip the dewclaws, which are equivalent to the nails on the human thumb.

If you do accidentally cut the quick, don't panic—although your cat will certainly complain. Apply styptic powder to the cut (you can get the powder at any pharmacy or pet supply store, and it's a good idea to have it on hand), or apply direct pressure to the bleeding nail for five minutes.

If the cat protests so much that you can't cut its nails even with someone else to hold it, leave the job to a professional.

Even conscientious owners often overlook the
care of their cat's teeth. If you have a kitten, watch
for it to begin replacing its front baby teeth when
it's three or four months old. At this time, you may
see blood on the gums or empty spaces. It's unlikely that your kitten will have any teething problems, but if you have any concern, consult the
veterinarian.

The teeth of adult cats often develop stains and
dental calculus (commonly called tartar), which
are deposits located on the teeth at the gumline. If
the tartar is allowed to accumulate, it will cause
bacteria to form under the gum, and this will lead
to pyorrhea (the accumulation of pus along the
root of the tooth) and eventual tooth loss. Mouth
odor is a sure sign of decay, infection, or a dietary
problem, so any time your cat has "bad breath,"
have your veterinarian check it out.

Tartar accumulation is due to food accumulation
and lack of surface action on the teeth when the
cat eats. If the accumulation of tartar seems to be
excessive, the cat's diet should be discussed with
your veterinarian. Never give a cat bones because
you think they'll clean the teeth. The bones may
splinter and injure the cat.

If you have children, you probably figure you
have enough trouble getting the kids to brush their
teeth without having to worry about the cat, too.
Regular toothbrushing, however, will do wonders
to help keep your cat's mouth healthy. Not all cats
will allow you to clean their teeth, but if you are
lucky enough to have an accommodating cat that
will allow this procedure, take advantage of its

good nature and clean its teeth once a week. You can use either a child's toothbrush, a gauze pad, or a pet finger brush. Rub the teeth and gums vigorously, especially the side premolars and molars. Use of a pet toothpaste is beneficial for proper cleaning. Professional dental cleaning needs to be done also—just like with humans.

Hairballs

Cats groom themselves by licking their fur, and this often causes hairballs. The cat's tongue is covered with many small barbs that make the tongue feel like sandpaper to the touch. As the cat licks itself, hair gets caught on the barbs and is swallowed.

If enough hair collects in the stomach without passing into the intestinal tract, the cat will try to vomit in an effort to get rid of it. A vomited hairball often looks like a long cigar. If there is more hair in the stomach that the cat can vomit up, it'll vomit its food—there is no room for food in the stomach because the stomach is full of hair. The cat will act normally and be hungry; it may try to eat the vomited food.

The best way to treat hairballs is to give the cat an agent that coats the stomach, combining with the hair to permit it to pass into the intestine and then out of the body in the stool. White petroleum jelly is an excellent coating substance. Some cats like the taste and will lick it right off the spoon; otherwise, you can easily place a teaspoonful or two of the jelly on the cat's mouth and paws so that the cat will lick it off. If your cat doesn't cooperate with this treatment, you can get a commercial preparation of flavored petroleum jelly from your vet or pet supply store. This may go down better with your cat. The treatment should be repeated daily until both the jelly and the hair are passed in the stool and the cat stops vomiting.

It is important to realize that if the cat is generally lethargic and has no appetite, or if the vomiting continues for more than two or three days, the problem is probably something other than hairballs. In this case, the cat needs veterinary attention as soon as possible.

VACCINATION: A KEY TO GOOD HEALTH

Just as vaccinations now protect children from conditions that used to be killers, scientists have discovered ways to vaccinate cats against a number of once fatal diseases. Vaccinations are a routine part of your preventive medicine schedule for your cat, and the first time you meet your veterinarian on a professional basis will probably be when you take your cat or kitten for these shots.

How Vaccination Works

In both humans and animals, the body is protected against disease by substances called antibodies that are carried in the white blood cells. These antibodies form in response to the presence of a specific disease-causing microorganism in the body, and they're able to fight and kill the invader. One way to develop immunity is to contract the disease and recover from it. Since this is neither practical nor desirable, vaccination is used to protect against some diseases.

Vaccination involves injecting into the body a vaccine—a preparation containing the microorganism that causes the disease against which protection is required. The microorganism in the vaccine, however, has been biologically altered so that it

cannot actually cause disease. The body responds
to the vaccine as if the disease were present, and
forms protective antibodies to fight it. This protection, in some cases, can last a lifetime. In other
cases, the vaccination must be repeated at intervals
(usually annually) to maintain its effect.

Don't assume that because you plan for your cat
to lead a sheltered life, it doesn't need to be vaccinated. Veterinarians hear this all too often and
point out that a bigger myth couldn't exist. The
best analogy is that of a bed-ridden person who
lives alone and who never leaves the house, yet still
gets sick. The viruses and bacteria that cause illness
in both people and in cats are easily spread either
in the air or on shoes and clothing, and no cat is
safe from diseases like feline panleukopenia (distemper) unless it has received the appropriate
vaccination.

All kittens receive a certain amount of natural or
acquired immunity to disease from their mother.
The protective antibodies are passed to the kittens
in the first milk—called colostrum—in the first 24
hours of life. This protection, however, is short-
lived, depending in part on how well-protected the
mother was before the birth of the litter. Some
kittens receive very little protection and are susceptible to disease as early as six to eight weeks
after birth; most kittens lose all this acquired immunity by the time they are 14 to 16 weeks old.
The veterinarian, therefore, starts vaccinating
kittens when they're between six and eight weeks
old. Your veterinarian will work out a suitable
schedule for your particular cat and the complete

program will cover the following infectious diseases:

Feline panleukopenia (distemper)
Feline viral rhinotracheitis (FVR)
Feline calicivirus (FCV)
Feline chlamydiosis (pneumonitis)
Rabies
Feline infectious peritonitis (FIP)
Feline leukemia virus (FeLV)

These diseases are explained below.

Feline Panleukopenia (Distemper)

Panleukopenia (commonly referred to as distemper) is a highly contagious viral disease of cats. It's caused by a parvovirus that is transmitted through the vomit, stool, or urine of an infected cat.

Signs and diagnosis. Early signs of infection include lack of appetite and vomiting, which will lead to dehydration, fever, and general lethargy. Diarrhea often follows these early signs. Panleukopenia in kittens is frequently fatal; older cats are usually resistant to infection either because they've been previously exposed to the virus without serious consequences, or because of vaccinations. However, it is not unusual to see older cats who have not been vaccinated contract this disease. Diagnosis is based on the clinical signs and on the results of blood tests. A cat that has a very low white blood cell count accompanied by diarrhea and vomiting probably has panleukopenia.

Treatment. Treatment of panleukopenia is a complex procedure involving fluid therapy to correct dehydration, antibiotics to control secondary bacterial invaders, and specific medications to treat such symptoms as diarrhea and vomiting.

Prevention. If the female cat (queen) is properly vaccinated before she is bred, she will impart good temporary immunity to the kittens. For solid protection, kittens should be vaccinated at eight to 10 weeks, then at three-weekly intervals up to 14 to 16 weeks. Older cats must be boostered each year for continual protection. Remember, panleukopenia is not only a kitten disease—it can affect a cat at any age.

Feline Viral Rhinotracheitis (FVR)

Feline viral rhinotracheitis (FVR) is probably one of the most serious and contagious respiratory infections a cat can contract. It's caused by a herpes virus that affects the upper respiratory tract, and the virus is transmitted in all the respiratory secretions.

Signs and diagnosis. Signs of FVR vary, but the disease usually causes sneezing, coughing, runny eyes and nose, fever, lethargy, heavy drooling, and lack of appetite. Often the eyes are involved, in which case the cat will squint and have a heavy mucous discharge from the eyes. If there's more than one cat in the household, they are all likely to show signs of disease at the same time. The veterinarian can usually make a diagnosis on the basis of the clinical signs. Laboratory isolation of the virus is possible, but it's time-consuming and costly.

Treatment. Treatment of FVR involves the use of broad-spectrum antibiotics (medications that are effective against a large number of infections) to combat secondary infection. The cat's eyes are treated with antibiotics; if the eyes develop a herpes ulcer, special medication is called for. Intensive supportive therapy is also necessary—intravenous fluid therapy, forced feeding, and sometimes blood transfusions as well. This supportive therapy maintains the cat while its body's own defenses fight the virus; without this treatment, the cat will certainly die from dehydration and starvation. Even with the most careful nursing, the cat may not survive.

Prevention. If you've ever seen a cat with FVR, you'll never hesitate to have your own cats vaccinated; it is a terrible illness. Fortunately, after many years of research, there is now available a vaccine that has cut the incidence of FVR way down. The vaccine is frequently combined with the panleukopenia and calicivirus vaccines; all three are given together, first when the kitten is seven to eight weeks old, and then at three-weekly intervals until 14 to 16 weeks. Older cats should get annual boosters.

Feline Calicivirus (FCV)

Calicivirus is also a highly contagious disease of cats and can cause signs similar to those of feline viral rhinotracheitis (FVR). Calicivirus is transmitted in the respiratory secretions of an infected cat.

Signs and diagnosis. Like FVR, signs of calicivirus include sneezing, coughing, runny eyes and nose, fever, lethargy, heavy drooling, and lack of appetite. If the eyes are involved, the cat squints and has a heavy mucous discharge from the eyes.

Calicivirus can also cause sores on the mouth and tongue. Calicivirus is not so often fatal as FVR, but it is extremely contagious. Diagnosis is made on the basis of the clinical signs. The virus can be isolated in the laboratory, but this process is expensive and time-consuming.

Treatment. Broad-spectrum antibiotics that fight a variety of infections are used to treat secondary infection. Intensive supportive therapy is also necessary, and may include intravenous fluid therapy, forced feeding, and sometimes blood transfusions. Without this intensive care, a cat with severe calicivirus infection will not survive, but will die from starvation and dehydration.

Prevention. The calicivirus vaccine has proven very effective in controlling this serious disease. It's given as a 3-in-1 vaccination with the panleukopenia and FVR vaccines, first when the kitten is eight to 10 weeks old, then at three-weekly intervals until 14 to 16 weeks. Older cats must be boostered annually.

Feline Chlamydiosis (Pneumonitis)

This disease is not nearly as dangerous as FVR or calicivirus, but it does cause a disturbing upper respiratory infection, especially in cats that are housed together with a lot of other cats. Pneumonitis is not caused by a virus but by a chlamydial organism (something between a bacterium and a virus). It's transmitted through respiratory tract secretions—sneezing, for example.

Signs and diagnosis. Signs of pneumonitis are usually limited to sneezing and mild watering of

77

the eyes. The veterinarian diagnoses pneumonitis by observing the clinical signs. A cat with a mild respiratory infection that has no fever and continues to eat is usually assumed to have pneumonitis.

Treatment. Because this is not a viral condition, antibiotics are often useful in treating pneumonitis. Supportive therapy may include eye drops to treat eye infection, antibiotics to try to destroy the organism and control secondary bacterial invaders, forced feeding if necessary, and occasionally intravenous fluid therapy if signs of dehydration are present.

Prevention. Routine vaccination against pneumonitis is not generally necessary for house cats. However, if you've got a number of cats, if your cat goes outside, or if you exhibit your cat in breed shows, you should discuss the advisability of vaccination with your veterinarian. The cat is vaccinated at eight to 10 weeks, is vaccinated again at 14 to 16 weeks, and needs annual boosters.

Rabies

Rabies is one animal disease that everyone knows about. It's caused by a virus that affects the brain and, while all warm-blooded animals are susceptible, the animals most commonly affected in North America are dogs, cats, bats, foxes, raccoons, and skunks. The incidence of rabies is not as high in cats as in dogs, but it is increasing. The disease is transmitted by direct contact with the saliva of an infected animal. Because humans can be infected by contact with a rabid animal, domestic animals must by law be vaccinated against the disease.

78

Rabies laws are strictly enforced throughout the United States. Hawaii, England, and other countries are free of rabies because of strict quarantine laws and natural protection, like a body of water that prevents migration of the virus.

Signs and diagnosis. Most cats will exhibit the furious form of rabies which, as the name implies, manifests itself as vicious behavior that makes the cat attack anything in its way. The cat usually dies within 10 days of the appearance of the signs of rabies. If a cat is suspected of having rabies, it must be destroyed and its brain checked for presence of the virus; this is the only way of confirming the diagnosis.

Treatment. If examination of the cat's brain reveals that the animal did have rabies, any person who had been bitten by the cat or exposed to its saliva must undergo rabies shots. The new human diploid-cell rabies vaccine, now used in people who have been exposed to a rabid animal, replaces the painful series of shots that used to be given. Early intervention is important. If the diploid-cell vaccine is given before signs of rabies appear, the success rate is high. It's possible but rare for the vaccine, correctly used, to save the person once he or she shows signs of the disease.

Prevention. The cat must be vaccinated, first at four months of age and then every year for the rest of its life. Certain rabies vaccines will protect the cat for up to three years, but the decision to use these vaccines must be determined by local laws and your veterinarian. If you ever suspect that your cat or any other animal has rabies, try to confine the animal without touching it—never touch an animal that may be rabid with your bare hands—and call the proper authorities. Usually it is only necessary to call the law enforcement agency for your district.

Feline Infectious Peritonitis (FIP)

Infectious peritonitis in cats was first described in 1953 and was not fully researched until 1963, at which point its highly contagious nature was discovered. The virus that causes infectious peritonitis is a coronavirus (the name comes from its shape). This virus, which is found also in other species, attacks the gastrointestinal tract and the respiratory system. The virus is contagious from cat to cat via all body secretions.

Signs and diagnosis. Signs of infection vary, and the disease appears to progress in two phases. The first phase may be mild signs of an upper respiratory problem, such as sneezing and discharges from the eyes and nose. At this stage, the cat usually responds to antibiotic therapy, but then regresses to the second phase of the disease which is represented by an increase in temperature, lethargy, lack of appetite, and pain in the abdomen. Examination may reveal that both the abdomen and the chest are full of fluid, causing great difficulty in breathing. This is called the "wet form" of FIP and represents about 50 percent of cases of the disease. In the other 50 percent of cases, the cat has no fluid accumulation in the abdomen or chest but has a fever that does not respond to antibiotics. This form of the disease can also manifest itself as seizures, eye problems, and kidney disease. Diagnosis is based on the clinical signs and results of supporting blood tests. The common antibody titer test is not conclusive evidence that the cat has FIP but, rather, exposure to one of several corona viruses. Research is underway to develop an FIP-specific test.

Treatment. The veterinarian should see the animal as soon as possible in order to make a diagnosis. However, treatment of FIP is seldom successful. The cat's body cannot produce enough antibodies to kill the virus, and the virus affects all the organs, especially the liver. FIP is usually fatal.

Prevention. The FIP virus is not very stable outside the cat's body and is easily destroyed by household disinfectants. Household bleach diluted 1:32 with water will kill the FIP virus. An infected cat should be separated from any other cats in the household and should use separate food dishes and litter pan. If your cat should die from FIP, don't introduce a new cat into the house for at least one week after disinfecting. If there is any sign of illness in any cat at home, a new cat should not be introduced until the diagnosis has been made, treatment of the other cats started if necessary, and the veterinarian has stated that it's safe to bring in the new cat. It's important to note that a safe and effective vaccine is now available to prevent FIP.

Feline Leukemia Virus (FeLV)

Leukemia is the term used to describe cancer of the blood cells, although it is a much more complicated matter than this definition seems to imply.

What you need to remember is that it is cancer, and that the unique thing about this type of cancer in cats is that it's caused by a retrovirus that is highly contagious between cats. Infected cats excrete high levels of the virus in their saliva and blood, and it is through exposure to these substances that infection is transmitted from one cat to another.

Signs and diagnosis. Signs of leukemia vary but the most common signs are anemia (low red blood cell count), weight loss, persistent fever, frequent respiratory disease, difficulty breathing, and "fading kitten syndrome"—a state in which kittens become progressively weaker and die. Diagnosis is based on the signs of the disease and the results of blood tests.

Treatment. So far, there is no successful treatment for feline leukemia. Various anti-cancer drugs have been tried but the results have been disappointing. The type of leukemia will dictate whether treatment can be tried or not.

Prevention. Certain cats can be carriers of the leukemia virus yet show no signs of illness themselves. These cats present a constant risk to healthy cats, and for this reason all cats that are in contact with other cats should be tested for presence of the virus. There are two excellent blood tests that will reveal the leukemia virus, and these tests should be run on all stray cats and on cats in multiple cat households, shelters, and catteries. If tests reveal that a cat is a carrier, that cat should be isolated to prevent spread of the disease.

Some researchers feel that the virus may be contagious to humans, and that carrier cats may constitute a public health hazard. Although no evidence exists at the moment to indicate any threat to humans, the possibility should be acknowledged.

A vaccine is currently available for prevention of FeLV infection. The decision to vaccinate should be made between the cat owner and the veterinarian. The vaccine is safe and very effective and will help in curbing this devastating disease.

Other Diseases

Feline Immunodeficiency Virus (FIV)

Feline immunodeficiency virus is a newly recognized virus in cats. Although similar to the feline leukemia virus (FeLV), FIV is not associated with cancer. This virus suppresses the body's immune system, causing secondary infections.

Signs and diagnosis. Because of the nature of the virus, all the signs of FIV are limited to secondary infections. Fevers of unknown origin, chronic bladder infections and upper respiratory infections, infections of the gums, chronic diarrhea, and anemia are all possibilities. Diagnosis is usually based on blood testing. Positive cats should be assumed to be contagious to other cats. The mode of infection is through saliva and blood (body secretions).

Treatment. Treatment of FIV is aimed at supportive care for all the secondary diseases listed above. Cats with FIV seem to get worse with time as the immune system weakens.

Prevention. Prevention is aimed at avoiding contact with infected cats. If your cat is kept indoors, it is virtually impossible for it to get the virus. Body secretions are the mode of transfer, and most cats that are infected get the virus through fighting with an FIV-positive cat.

Ringworm (Fungal Infection)

One of the most infectious skin diseases in cats is ringworm (dermatophytosis). Ringworm fungi live on the surface of the skin and are very contagious from cat to cat and from cat to man. Typically, the long-haired cat, such as the Persian, will contract ringworm as a kitten and sometimes will go unnoticed until the owner breaks out with lesions. Classically, the lesions on cats are circular areas with hair loss, short hairs, and scaling. Treatment is designed at preventing spread. Oral medications, anti-fungal shampoos, fur clipping, and environmental cleaning are all undertaken to control the spread. An infected cat needs to have veterinary attention to cure the problem.

Zoonoses—Diseases Transmitted From Cat To Man

The following is a list of diseases possibly transmitted from cat to human. Immunosuppressed individuals will be much more susceptible and should take precaution.

• Toxoplasma gondii is a protozoan parasite (one-celled organism) that can cause a neurologic disease in humans. People may contract this disease by eating uncooked or raw meat, ingesting the organism from cat feces, or transplacental transmission. Pregnant women must take precautions by wearing gloves when working in the garden and cleaning the cat box. (See the section "Toxoplasmosis" for more details.)

• "Cat scratch disease (fever)" is a bacterial disease carried by the cat that will cause enlargement of the lymph nodes in humans. The causative organism has been recently identified as Rochalimaea henselae. "Cat scratch disease" is usually mild and does not recur. It is advisable to wash cuts, bites, and scratches promptly with soap and water and not let a cat lick any open wounds on your body.

• Rabies is probably the most serious zoonotic disease. If a cat contracts rabies and bites a human, it is likely that the human will get rabies. Vaccination of cats is mandatory in most areas of the United States and should be given annually or as often as determined by local laws and your veterinarian.

• Campylobacter is a bacterial disease of the intestine that causes diarrhea and is contagious to humans.

• Chlamydiosis is a disease that causes sneezing in cats. It has been shown that the causative organism can cause conjunctivitis in humans.

• Salmonellosis is an intestinal disease caused by a bacteria. It causes diarrhea and is contagious to humans.

• Ringworm is a fungal disease of the skin that causes hair loss. Humans are susceptible to it and will develop skin lesions that become itchy.

85

PARASITES THAT BUG YOUR CAT

Parasites are a problem that most cat owners have to deal with at one time or another. Parasites are, by definition, organisms that survive by feeding off another creature, and the two types that may select your cat as their host are external parasites that live in or on the skin or in the ear canals, and internal parasites that inhabit the internal organs—usually the intestines.

External parasites all resemble insects, and some are so small that they cannot be seen with the naked eye and must be put under a microscope for identification. The external parasites most commonly found on cats are fleas, ticks, lice, mange mites, and ear mites. Most of them are highly contagious, and if one cat in a household is infected, other cats in the same household are likely to be infected, too. These parasites cause severe itching, skin infections, and loss of hair. You can control external parasites with insecticides that you use both on the animal and on the environment—many of these pests live part of their life off the cat in the grass of your lawn or in convenient nooks and crannies in your home. The medication you use will depend on the type of parasite you're dealing with, and your veterinarian can identify the problem and suggest a suitable insecticide.

The most common internal parasites live in the cat's intestines, and if they're left untreated they can cause serious problems like chronic diarrhea, anemia (red blood cell deficiency), poor condition of coat, and cough. Some internal parasites attack other organs, like the heart or lungs. All cats are susceptible to internal parasites.

Unlike some external parasites, which you may (after some experience of cat ownership) be able to identify and treat yourself with a topical product such as a flea powder, internal parasites always require professional veterinary attention. Although you should be able to recognize the signs of a possible problem, you should never try to diagnose or treat internal parasites yourself. Your veterinarian will make the diagnosis by examining a sample of the cat's feces under a microscope. In most cases, the veterinarian is looking not for the parasite itself but for the minute eggs that the organism deposits in the stool. Once the diagnosis is made, the veterinarian will prescribe the appropriate medication. Don't ever medicate for internal parasites without professional advice; worming medicines are poisons and should never be administered at random.

The internal parasites that most commonly infect the cat's intestines are roundworms, hookworms, tapeworms, coccidia, and toxoplasmosis. The potentially very dangerous heartworm, a parasite once thought to affect only dogs, is now being found also in cats. Heartworm is found in the heart, not the intestines.

The following discussion of individual parasites will help you recognize the signs of parasitic infestation.

External Parasites

Fleas

Fleas are tiny brown insects that live on the cat's skin and feed by sucking the animal's blood. If you part the cat's fur, you can see them moving. Fleas can't fly, but they can jump quite a distance and travel easily from one cat to another. They irritate the skin and make the cat scratch—although not all scratching cats have fleas. The saliva of the flea is a potent allergen that can set up a severe allergic reaction in a susceptible cat. In such a case, the cat will lose a great deal of hair, especially above the tail, and develop scaly skin on its back. It will probably scratch itself so persistently that the skin bleeds. This condition is known as fleabite dermatitis. Besides irritating the skin, the flea is the intermediate host of the tapeworm—an internal parasite that is described later in this chapter.

In some parts of the United States, fleas are a year-round problem. In the Northern climates, the winter cold will kill fleas outdoors; they can, however, live comfortably in your home.

Life cycle. The adult flea lays its eggs on the cat or in the environment—on the lawn, in the cat's bed, or in your carpet. The eggs laid on the cat fall off and, after a period that varies from two to 12 days depending on environmental temperature and humidity, hatch into legless larvae—the immature form of the insect. After feeding for nine to 100 days on the ground, the larvae spin cocoons in which they remain for five days to one year—again, the length of time depends on environmental conditions. The adult fleas emerge from the cocoons and hop onto the cat. The female fleas reproduce almost immediately.

Signs and diagnosis. The most common indication that a cat has fleas is extreme itching. But don't assume that the itching is caused by fleas unless you actually see them. Spread the cat's fur on the rump or in the groin and look for the adult fleas running through the fur. Another way to check is to rub the animal's rump vigorously onto a wet, white paper towel. Flea feces are mostly blood, and any black specks that fall on the towel and smear to a reddish-brown color are evidence of flea infestation. As mentioned earlier, an allergic reaction to prolonged exposure to the fleas' saliva may cause hair loss, scaliness on the back, and raw patches where the cat has scratched itself.

Control and treatment. Control of fleas can be a wearisome business. You'll need the advice of your veterinarian and, possibly, an exterminator. You must treat the affected cat and all the other animals in the household, and you must also treat the animal's indoor and, in some cases, outdoor environment. If the cat has scratched itself raw, cortisone given orally or by injection should clear up the condition.

A number of cat shampoos and dips are available that will effectively kill the fleas. Sprays and powders are quick and effective. With any product, read the manufacturer's instructions carefully before using the product on the cat; some insecticides that are effective for dogs are not safe for cats. It's best to ask your veterinarian to recommend a product, and then to use it strictly according to the manufacturer's instructions. Remember, also, that any insecticide you use on your pet can cause side effects like vomiting, excess salivation, or skin irritation. Check before you use the product that you know what to do if there are side effects. A flea collar can be very effective if used properly and can help keep the animal from becoming reinfested. Remember that a flea collar is a method of control, not necessarily a ridding device.

Insect growth regulators (IGRs) should be used to stop the life cycle of the flea. These chemicals were developed to interfere with the second-stage larva and prevent it from further developing into the adult. Further research indicates that IGRs may also prevent the egg from hatching by affecting the adult female. IGRs have revolutionized the flea fighting industry. Using IGRs with adulticides in the environment and ridding the cat of adult fleas are sure ways to stop the pest.

Once you've treated the animal or animals, thoroughly clean the house, the cat's sleeping place (or places), and any other areas where the fleas may breed. Your veterinarian can recommend an insecticide, frequently a spray, that will fog the infested area.

Ticks

Ticks are small, insect-like creatures that usually inhabit the parts of the cat where the hair is thin. They bury their heads in the skin and suck the animal's blood. Although they can be found anywhere on the body, they seem to prefer the head area, especially around the ears. When they are swollen with blood, ticks are about the size of a pea. Usually, the only result of a tick bite is mild irritation.

Life cycle. After gorging itself on the cat's blood, the female tick drops off and lays its eggs in a crack or crevice, indoors or outdoors, where they incubate and then hatch into larvae or "seed ticks." These attach themselves to the cat and feed on the blood, then fall to the ground and, after a week or two, molt to their next stage of development—the nymph stage. Again, they find the cat, feed, fall off, and molt to the adult stage. The adult male and female ticks mate, and the cycle repeats.

Signs and diagnosis. The signs of tick infection aren't always as obvious as you might expect. The cat won't usually scratch excessively, and unless you actually see and remove them, the ticks can live a long and comfortable life. The best way of keeping your animal clear of this parasite is to check the skin regularly around the head, ears, and neck, under the arms, and in any other thin-haired area.

Control and treatment. As with fleas, getting rid of ticks involves treating both the cat and its surroundings. If there are only a few ticks on the animal—as is usually the case with a cat—remove them with tweezers. Use the tweezers to grasp the tick where its head is embedded in the skin, and pull the tick out. Destroy the tick after removal. Try to remove the whole tick; if the head is left embedded in the cat's skin, it may cause a sore. Don't ever use a cigarette to remove a tick from the cat's skin, because you'll almost certainly burn the cat.

If your cat is heavily infected, bathe it with an insecticidal solution recommended by your veterinarian. Put a tick collar on the cat and use sprays or powders periodically, as directed by the veterinarian, to help keep the animal free of further tick problems.

When you've treated the cat, treat the environment. You can use an insecticide to fog your home. Sprays are also available to use in your yard, on the lawn, on woodpiles, or in other areas where the ticks may be hiding.

Lice

Lice are tiny wingless insects, barely visible to the naked eye, that live their entire life cycle on the cat. There are a number of different types of lice, but each type is host-specific—that is, it can only live on one species of animal. Cat lice live only on cats and can't survive on dogs or humans; human lice don't infect animals. The lice pass from one host to another by direct contact and can be found on all parts of the body.

Life cycle. The female lice lay eggs on the cat but, unlike the flea eggs that fall off the animal, these eggs (or nits) are attached to the hair shaft. They are small, white particles and look a bit like dandruff. The parasite lives out its life and reproductive cycle on the cat.

Signs and diagnosis. The signs of infection are usually limited to itching. If the infestation is severe, the cat may scratch itself raw. The veterinarian will look for the lice eggs on the cat and may examine some of the cat's hairs under the microscope for the presence of the eggs.

Control and treatment. It's important to have lice identified by your veterinarian, but treatment is straightforward and successful. Lice are easier to get rid of than some of the other external parasites. Because they live out their full cycle on the cat, it's only necessary to treat the animal. If there's more than one cat in the family, however, it is necessary to treat them all.

Your veterinarian can recommend a cat shampoo, dip, or spray to get rid of the lice. You'll probably have to repeat the treatment at weekly intervals for three weeks. Note that some insecticides that can be used on dogs are *not* safe for use on cats, so read the label on the product carefully and follow instructions. If the cat has scratched itself raw, the veterinarian will prescribe a medication such as cortisone to heal the lesions.

Mange Mites

Mites are small, insect-like parasites that spend their whole life cycle on the cat and will live only a short time off the animal. They are very small and can't be seen without a microscope. Like lice, mange mites are host-specific. Most animal species are susceptible to some type of mange mite, but the types that affect cats won't affect dogs or people, and vice versa. Of the several types that affect cats, the most common are notoedric and demodectic mites. Each type is described separately below.

93

Notoedric Mange

Notoedric mange is classified as a sarcoptid mite. This highly contagious mite causes severe head lesions in cats, starting at the tips of the ears and spreading to the whole head. If this condition is left untreated, the whole body may become infected.

Life cycle. The female mite tunnels into the skin and lays eggs that hatch in 10 to 14 days. The cat hosts the mites for their entire life cycle.

Signs and diagnosis. The signs of notoedric mange vary, but the most common are scaliness and loss of hair around the ears and on the head. Intense itching is a characteristic of this condition. Your veterinarian diagnoses notoedric mange by scraping a suspected lesion and examining it under a microscope for the presence of the mite or its eggs. Skin scrapings, however, do not always reveal the presence of the culprit—especially if the condition is caught in its early stages—and here it's possible that you may be able to help. If you have developed small marks similar to mosquito bites on your own body, the mange mite may be responsible. Although the mite cannot live on humans, it will bite.

Control and treatment. Your veterinarian will prescribe an insecticide to cure notoedric mange. You'll probably need to apply the medication weekly for three weeks to get rid of the mites completely, and all cats in the household must be treated at the same time. Long-haired cats that are severely infected should be clipped before treatment. Your vet can prescribe medications to control itching and prevent further skin infection.

Demodectic Mange

This type of mange is often called "red mange" and is caused by a microscopic mite that has an elongated shape and lives deep in the skin in hair follicles. Demodectic mange can be localized to one or two areas of the cat's body or generalized over the whole body. Demodectic mange is less common in cats than in dogs.

Life cycle. The only way demodectic mange mites can be transferred is from the mother to the kitten at birth. The mite's life cycle in the cat is not fully understood.

Signs and diagnosis. Hair loss is the first indicator of demodectic mange. In severe cases, secondary bacterial infections can cause the skin to become thickened and inflamed. Sometimes, but not always, the cat will scratch to relieve itching caused by the condition. Your veterinarian can diagnose the demodectic mange only from microscopic examination of skin scrapings.

Control and treatment. Many insecticidal preparations have been put forward as cures for demodectic mange, but, in fact, treatment has often proved very disappointing. Localized lesions often respond well to treatment, but generalized demodectic mange has always been very frustrating to the owner and the veterinarian. Since recovery often depends on the body's own defense mechanism, the cat must be in top shape for the defense mechanism (antibodies) to work properly.

Ear Mites

Ear mites, often called "ear mange," are insect-like creatures that resemble the notoedric mange mites. They live in the ear canal—hence the name—and can barely be seen with the naked eye.

Life cycle. The ear mite lives its whole life in the ear canal. Occasionally, a few travel to other parts of the body, but these wanderers don't seem to cause any problems. The mite is host-specific and is highly contagious between animals of the same species.

Signs and diagnosis. Several clues can warn you that your cat has ear mites. Head-shaking and intense itching are often the first signs (but these signs can also indicate ear problems other than mites). Often there's a brown, waxy material in the ears, and if a secondary infection has set in, the ear canal will emit an unpleasant odor.

Control and treatment. Ear mites respond well to treatment, and in many cases you won't even need to see the veterinarian. Thorough daily cleaning of the ears with cotton swabs is a must (the grooming section tells you how to do it), and often plain mineral oil dropped in the ears after every cleaning is enough to kill the mites. This daily cleaning should be continued for 10 to 14 days. However, if the cat is still obviously distressed after a few days, see a veterinarian. If one cat in the household has ear mites, you must treat all the animals in the house at the same time, even if their ears don't seem to be infected, and repeat the treatment daily for 10 to 14 days.

If the smell of the ears indicates that a secondary

infection has set in, your veterinarian will prescribe an antibiotic ointment.

Dandruff Mite (Cheyletiella)

This parasite is known as the dandruff mite because it looks like human dandruff. It lives on the surface of the skin, and if you look closely, you can see the white, speck-like insects move. The parasite is highly contagious by contact between one cat and another.

Life cycle. The dandruff mite lives its entire life cycle on the cat and will not live for very long off the animal.

Signs and diagnosis. Intense itching is the cat's basic reaction to dandruff mite infection (although not all scratching cats have dandruff mites). If the cat is scratching and you can see the moving white specks, you can be pretty sure what the problem is.

Control and treatment. The dandruff mite doesn't present as many problems as some other external parasites. It's easily destroyed by the use of commonly used miticides available from the veterinarian. This parasite is often seen in catteries and other high-density areas. In order to keep the problem from spreading, the affected cat or cats should be treated and isolated until they are free of the mites.

Internal Parasites

Roundworms

These are long, white worms that look like spaghetti, and they're easy to recognize in the cat's stool or vomit. It's probably safe to assume that most kittens will contract roundworms from their mother, but older cats usually become resistant to them. Under normal sanitary conditions, these parasites are not such a serious problem as other, faster-developing parasites.

Because the roundworm larvae can infect humans, this parasite is regarded as a public health hazard. In humans, however, the roundworm infects not the intestine but the liver or the eyes.

Life cycle. The most common method of infection is through the uterus of the mother cat. Scientists have learned that the dormant, microscopic larvae present in the mother become active when she's about 42 days pregnant. The larvae (immature roundworms) migrate from the mother's tissues to those of the kittens while they are still in the uterus. After the kitten is born, the larvae either develop into adult worms in the kitten's intestine, or remain dormant in the tissues and become active when the kitten is older. In the case of a female, these dormant larvae will become active during her pregnancy and, in turn, infect her kittens. Another method of infection is through the mother's milk.

Signs and diagnosis. Kittens heavily infected with roundworms are thin and usually have diarrhea. Sometimes they look pot-bellied, but this by itself isn't sufficient proof of infection. Often you'll know for sure because the kitten passes the spaghetti-like worms in the stool, or vomits them up. Your veterinarian makes the diagnosis by analyzing the stool.

Control and treatment. The best method of control is to have stool samples checked periodically. If there's a problem, remove the infected stools immediately after the cat defecates in order to avoid reinfection, and worm the cat according to your veterinarian's recommendation.

Because roundworm larvae can infect humans, you should take some precautions. The best and most responsible way of doing this is to not let your cat go outside unless you are sure it is free of this parasite. Since cats like to use the children's sandbox as a litter box, the sandbox should always be covered when not in use (your cat may not have roundworms, but someone else's cat may). It's also wise to wear gloves while working in the yard, or to wash your hands thoroughly afterwards.

Hookworms

Hookworms are small parasites (less than half an inch long) that affect cats of all ages, although young kittens seem to be more susceptible than older cats. The parasites live in the small intestine and attach themselves to the lining of the intestine. Hookworms are bloodsuckers, and if there are enough of them they can cause severe anemia (deficiency of red blood cells) and even death.

Life cycle. Under ideal hot and humid conditions, hookworm eggs passed in the stool of an infected cat incubate very quickly—within 24 hours—to the immature larva stage. All the cat has to do to become infected is walk on the soil where the eggs or larvae are present. The larvae can penetrate the skin directly, or the eggs can enter the cat's system when it licks them off its feet and swallows them.

Signs and diagnosis. As mentioned earlier, young kittens are particularly susceptible to hookworms. Young animals that are infected look very thin and their fur is scruffy and dull. Diarrhea tinged with blood is common in both young and older cats. The veterinarian diagnoses hookworms by microscopic examination of the stool for the parasite's eggs.

Control and treatment. Hookworm infestation is treated with medications specifically indicated for this parasite. Your veterinarian will set up a worming routine for your cat that will include medication as well as environmental clean-up. Remember that it can reinfect itself from its own stools. Your cat will become reinfected time and again, no matter how often you worm it, if its litter pan is not kept clean, or if it's allowed outside where the ground is infected. Having your veterinarian check stool samples regularly (frequency depends on the climate in your area) is the most practical method of controlling hookworms.

Tapeworms

Tapeworms are flat and got their name from their shape and their resemblance to pieces of tape. In fact, tapeworm segments passed in the cat's stool look like grains of rice. It's possible to see them moving as they are passed. Each segment is an egg packet containing a large number of eggs.

Life cycle. Unlike roundworms and hookworms, tapeworms are not transmitted directly from the stool. Tapeworm infection occurs when the cat eats an infected intermediate host—in this country, the flea is most likely to be the culprit. The flea has already fed on the tapeworm segments that contain the eggs and have been passed in the stool of an infected animal. Inside the flea, the eggs mature to the stage at which they can infect a cat. The flea lives in the cat's fur and, in the process of grooming itself, the cat swallows the flea. As the flea is digested, the eggs are released in the cat's intestine and grow to adult size. These adult tapeworms, in turn, lay eggs contained in segments that are passed in the cat's stool, and the cycle starts over. Mice, rabbits, and fish can also act as intermediate hosts for the tapeworm. So can cattle and pigs, and a cat that eats raw meat from any of these hosts can become infected.

Signs and diagnosis. Tapeworms seldom cause much real trouble beyond mild diarrhea and some rectal itching. You're most likely to spot them by examining the hair around the rectum for the rice-like segments that contain the tapeworm eggs, but because cats clean themselves so thoroughly, this is not always possible.

Control and treatment. As with so many parasite problems, treating tapeworms is a two-part task—you have to rid the cat of tapeworms and rid the environment of the intermediate host. Your veterinarian can treat the cat for tapeworms with an oral or injected medication. If the cat is getting the tapeworms from fleas, however, you won't make any progress unless you get rid of the fleas, too. The section on external parasites tells you how to do this.

Coccidia

Unlike the intestinal parasites discussed so far, this parasite is not a worm. It's a one-celled organism (protozoan) that lives in the intestine and usually causes problems in very young kittens. You can only see it under a microscope.

Life cycle. Coccidia multiply rapidly in the lining of the intestines and are transferred from one animal to another in the stool.

Signs and diagnosis. Very young kittens are usually most susceptible to coccidia, and this parasite is often found in kittens that have been housed with a lot of companions in unsanitary conditions. In breeding establishments, this parasite is often overlooked and consequently does not get treated. Typical warning signs are emaciated appearance and diarrhea that sometimes contains blood. Very often, secondary infections cause discharge from the eyes or nose.

Control and treatment. If it's not severe, coccidiosis is self-limiting and disappears when the surroundings are returned to a sanitary condition. However, medications are available, and your veterinarian can prescribe medication for the cat and make suggestions for maintaining a clean environment that will prevent the parasites from becoming established.

Toxoplasmosis

The toxoplasma organism is a one-celled protozoan parasite and is thought to be a member of the coccidia family. It can affect most species of warm-blooded animals but completes its life cycle in the cat only. The parasite lives in the intestines of the infected cat and usually causes no signs of disease; in fact, a large percentage of completely healthy domestic cats can be carriers of toxoplasmosis and can pass the infection to other animals and, in some cases, to humans.

The toxoplasma organism can cause a mild infection of the blood and other organs in human beings; usually the victim doesn't even realize he or she has the disease. However, an infected mother generally infects her unborn child, who risks damage to the brain and the eyes. A high percentage of babies born with toxoplasmosis will have a serious defect. It is fairly straightforward for a pregnant woman to avoid the risk of infection without getting rid of her cat, and these measures will be discussed under control and treatment.

Life cycle. Cats usually pick up toxoplasmosis from raw meat, especially from rats or mice that they have killed and eaten. The organism completes its life cycle in the cat's intestines.

Signs and diagnosis. As mentioned earlier, many cats harbor the toxoplasma organism with no ill effects. However, infection can occur and can affect the brain, liver, lungs, and eyes. A cat with this infection may show signs that include loss of appetite, lethargy, fever, and breathing difficulties. Initially, the veterinarian identifies toxoplasmosis through a fecal smear—a microscopic examination of a stool sample no more than 15 to 20 minutes old. If the cat shows signs of infection, a blood test can be performed to confirm the diagnosis.

Treatment and control. If the cat is sick, it can be treated with medication specifically indicated to kill the toxoplasma organism. Cats that are not showing any symptoms are not usually medicated. To prevent a cat from contracting toxoplasmosis, it should never be fed raw meat or allowed to kill rodents. If yours is an outdoor cat, however, what it does with its spare time is not under your control.

Note: In order to protect herself and her unborn baby from the risk of toxoplasmosis, a pregnant woman should take some simple precautions: She should never empty or clean the litterbox or touch the cat's feces with her bare hands—let someone else do the clean-up until after the baby is born; and she should wash her hands thoroughly after handling the cat or the cat's bedding, toys, or other belongings. The children's sandbox should be covered when not in use, and it's wise to wear gloves while working in the garden. As an added precaution, since toxoplasmosis can also be carried by meat animals, a pregnant woman should not eat rare or raw meat.

Heartworm

Heartworm disease was thought until recently to infect only dogs but is now being seen in cats, also. It's caused by a nematode (worm) that lives in its adult stage in the right side of the cat's heart. Heartworms are transmitted from one cat to another by mosquitoes and do all their damage in the adult stage, by which time the worms can be up to 12 inches long. Heartworm disease is a serious matter and can be fatal. Because the infection is transmitted by mosquitoes, heartworm disease used to be a real problem only in the warm, southern, coastal areas of the United States. Increased mobility of the population (and its pets) has caused the disease to spread widely.

Life cycle. There are three stages in the life cycle of the heartworm: 1) The adult female worm lays live, immature worms in the cat's bloodstream. 2) These immature worms can only develop further in the mosquito, so they remain in the cat's bloodstream until the animal is bitten by a mosquito. They then develop inside the mosquito to the infective larva stage; this process takes about two weeks. 3) The infected mosquito bites a cat and passes the infected larvae into the cat's bloodstream. The larvae live in the cat for about three months and then migrate to the cat's heart and settle in the right ventricle of the heart and the adjoining blood vessels. Within another three months, the worms are fully grown; they reproduce, and the cycle starts over.

Signs and diagnosis. Severe infection by adult heartworms can cause cough, breathing difficulties, fatigue, and general weakness. As the disease progresses, the cat's heart, liver, and lungs become severely damaged. Visible symptoms of the disease do not usually appear until the advanced stages, by which time the disease may be irreversible. Diagnosis of heartworm disease is based on the cat's history, clinical signs, chest X-rays, and blood tests to locate the presence of the parasite.

Control and treatment. Treatment of heartworm disease in cats is difficult and involves considerable risks. A medication available for dogs cannot currently be used for cats because its effects on the cat's system are unknown. Until further tests can be performed, prevention of mosquito bites is the only method of control available to cat owners.

Tests for heartworm are routinely carried out on dogs at intervals prescribed by the veterinarian according to the climate in the area. This, so far, has not been the case with cats, perhaps because so many of the cats seen by veterinarians are basically house pets that seldom go outside. The rising incidence of heartworm disease in cats, however, may lead to regular routine testing of cats, also.

Note that although heartworm disease has spread rapidly over the last 10 years, not all areas of the United States are heartworm areas. Your veterinarian can tell you if you live in, or are going to travel to, a heartworm area.

Hemobartonellosis (Feline Infectious Anemia)

Feline infectious anemia is caused by a small parasite *(hemobartonella felis)* which infects the red blood cells of the cat. Basically, the parasite destroys the red blood cells faster than the body can produce them. The mode of transmission from cat to cat is not clearly understood, but we do know that infected queens can transmit the parasite to their kittens. The parasite can also be transmitted by blood-sucking external parasites like fleas or ticks or in the course of a blood transfusion.

Signs and diagnosis. The most common clinical signs are lethargy, weakness, lack of appetite, and generally poor condition. Since many cat diseases have anemia as one of their signs, diagnosis is based on identifying the parasite in the red blood cells under the microscope.

Treatment. Treatment involves giving the antibiotic oxytetracycline orally for three weeks, and the recovery rate is excellent if the disease is caught in time. As the parasite is really never completely killed, cats that recover will be carriers indefinitely.

Prevention. Control of external parasites is one of the most important steps that can be taken in controlling this disease, and the section on external parasites tells you how to do this. Female cats should be checked before breeding for the presence of the parasite. A queen that is infected should not be bred.

Lungworm

This worm is found in cats worldwide and takes up residence in the cat's lungs. It's transmitted to the cat via a slug or snail.

Life cycle. In the cat's lungs, the female lungworm produces eggs that develop into larvae. These are coughed up from the lungs and the cat swallows them. The larvae are passed in the stool, enter a slug or snail, and develop within three to four weeks to the infective stage. At this point, any creature such as a frog, lizard, or snake that eats the infected slug or snail becomes a secondary host or carrier of the lungworm. This secondary host does not become infected itself; however, if it's eaten by a cat, it does pass the infection to the cat. Thus, the cat can contract lungworms directly from the infected slug or snail, or indirectly from the creature that has eaten the slug or snail.

Signs and diagnosis. Lungworm manifests its presence in the form of respiratory disease. The cat develops a chronic cough and breathing difficulties, loses its appetite, and becomes generally debilitated. Diagnosis is made through laboratory analyses of the cat's stool to reveal the infective larvae.

Control and treatment. Treatment involves oral medication to destroy the lungworm, but it's not highly successful. Prevention is better than cure, and the best way of lessening your cat's chance of getting lungworms is to not let it roam.

Dealing With An Emergency

Have you ever seen a cat injured in a fight or hit by a car? Perhaps you could only shake your head and walk away. Not because you didn't care, but because you didn't know how to approach and examine the animal, or what to do next. Especially if you have a cat of your own, you'll want to be prepared, for your pet depends on you for help in an emergency situation.

If we, like Dr. Doolittle, could "talk with the animals," it would be easy to find out what they'd gotten into, and where it hurt. But we can't, so in order to apply the proper treatment, we must be able to identify signs that pinpoint the problem. This chapter lists the most common emergencies alphabetically. When the nature of an injury or condition is not readily apparent, signs are listed at the beginning of the section to help you identify the problem.

The purpose of first aid is to relieve suffering and stabilize your cat's vital signs until professional help is obtained. This chapter will give you the information and techniques you'll need to confidently administer first aid and perhaps save the life of a pet. Clear directions are listed step-by-step. Where more than one procedure is necessary to perform a step, each specific action is described in substeps a, b, c, etc. The directions are further clarified with accompanying illustrations.

The "why" of these procedures is explained in the back of the chapter. This section also includes preventive measures that can eliminate or minimize some hazards that could be dangerous to your pet.

Because minutes count in an emergency situation, you'll want to have a first aid kit prepared. It needn't be elaborate; suggested items are listed on page 220. Keep the kit and this book together in a convenient place, and take both with you when you travel with your cat.

We suggest you take the time to thoroughly familiarize yourself with the contents of this chapter. Certain sections are especially important. When a cat is choking or unconscious, speed is vital if the cat is to live. Therefore, it is of primary importance that you know how to give artificial respiration and CPR (cardiopulmonary resuscitation). It will also be most helpful if you know exactly how to approach and restrain a cat if an accident does occur. The method of restraint that you choose will depend largely upon whether the cat is cooperative or uncooperative. It may become necessary for you to protect your own self from injury caused by an uncooperative cat's five weapons—its mouth and four sets of claws.

The following page provides space for important phone numbers, including the number for the Poison Control Center in your area. You will find them very helpful should it become necessary to contact them. The number is in your phone book.

EMERGENCY INFORMATION

VETERINARIAN'S
NAME:_____

EMERGENCY
PHONE:_____

HOSPITAL
PHONE:_____

HOSPITAL
ADDRESS:_____

POISON CONTROL
CENTER PHONE:_____

Approaching An Injured Cat

STEP 1: Approach slowly, speaking in a reassuring tone of voice.

STEP 2: Move close to the cat without touching it.

STEP 3: Stoop down to the cat. While continuing to speak, observe its eyes and body language.

a. If the cat is wide-eyed, ears back, growling, and hissing, DO NOT attempt to pet it. Proceed to RESTRAINING AN UNCOOPERATIVE CAT, page 118.

b. If the cat is shivering and crouching, attempt to reassure it by petting, first behind the head. If this is permitted, pet the rest of the head and neck. Scratching the ears and stroking under the chin is often comforting. Proceed to RESTRAINING A COOPERATIVE CAT, page 113.

> **CAUTION: A cat has five weapons: the mouth and four paws.**

Step 3b

Restraining A Cooperative Cat

A. IF YOU HAVE AN ASSISTANT

STEP 1: Place the cat in your arms or lap or on a table or other raised surface using one of the three following methods:

Method 1

a. Position yourself so the cat's head is to your left.

b. Reach with your right hand over the cat's body and under its chest so the chest is resting in your palm.

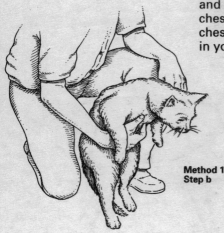

**Method 1
Step b**

CAUTION: A cat has five weapons: the mouth and four paws.

continued

c. Lift the cat firmly toward you so that its body is secured between your forearm and your body.

d. Grasp the top of the front legs with the fingers of your right hand, which is still supporting the chest.

e. Using the other hand, prevent the head from moving by grasping under the throat. Scratching the ears with this hand from under the throat is often very comforting.

f. Treatment can then be administered by your assistant while the cat is in your arms.

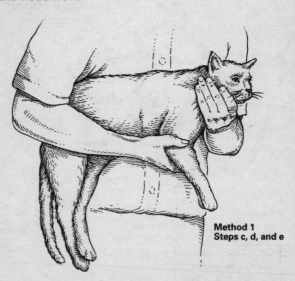

Method 1
Steps c, d, and e

114

Method 2

a. Grasp the loose
   skin on the back
   of the neck just
   below the ears.
   Lift the cat; most
   cats will become
   very submissive
   when this
   method is used.

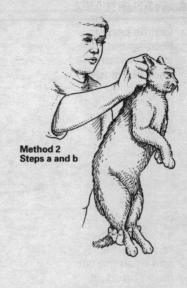

**Method 2
Steps a and b**

b. Grasp the hind
   legs with your
   other hand to
   prevent scratch-
   ing.

c. Still holding the
   cat, place it on a
   table, injured
   side up.

d. Pull forward on
   the skin of the
   neck and pull
   backward on the
   hind legs as if
   gently but firmly
   stretching
   the cat.

e. Have your
   assistant
   adminis-
   ter first
   aid.

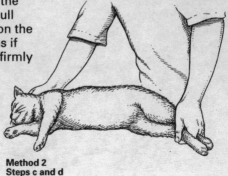

**Method 2
Steps c and d**

continued

Method 3

a. Lift the cat by holding the loose skin on the back of the neck in one hand and the loose skin of the back in the other.

**Method 3
Step a**

b. Place the cat on a table or other raised surface and push the cat down firmly; it will be unable to use its claws.

c. Have your assistant administer first aid.

**Method 3
Step b**

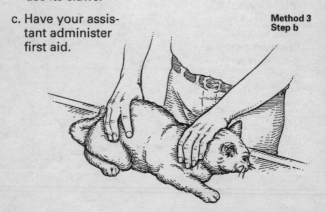

116

B. IF YOU ARE ALONE

CAUTION: A cat
has five weapons:
the mouth and
four paws.

STEP 1: Grasp the
loose skin on the
back of the neck just
below the ears.

STEP 2: Lift the cat
and place it on its
chest on a table or
other raised surface.

STEP 3: If the cat
will not stay, place it
in a large, open box.

STEP 4: Administer
first aid.

Step 1

Step 2

117

Restraining An Uncooperative Cat

A. IF YOU HAVE AN ASSISTANT

> CAUTION: A cat has five weapons: the mouth and four paws.

STEP 1: Drop a blanket or towel over the cat.

STEP 2: Scoop up the cat so the towel or blanket encompasses the entire cat, including all four paws.

Step 1

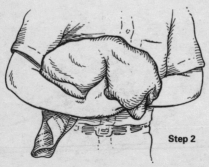

Step 2

STEP 3: Expose only the injured area, keeping the rest of the cat covered.

STEP 4: Have your assistant administer first aid. If the cat is still very aggressive, transport untreated, still covered in the blanket or towel, to the veterinarian.

Step 3

B. IF YOU ARE ALONE

CAUTION: A cat has five weapons: the mouth and four paws.

STEP 1: Drop a blanket or towel over the cat.

STEP 2: Scoop up the cat so the towel or blanket encompasses the entire cat, including all four paws.

STEP 3: Tie the ends of the towel or blanket together with cord to form a bag, or place the cat in a closed box.

STEP 4: DO NOT attempt to treat the injury. Transport to the veterinarian.

Step 2

119

Transporting An Injured Cat

A. IF THE CAT CAN BE LIFTED

STEP 1: If the cat is cooperative:

a. Position yourself so the cat's head is to your left.

b. Reach with your right hand over the cat's body and under its chest so the chest is resting in your palm.

c. Lift the cat firmly toward you so that its body is secured between your forearm and your body.

d. Grasp the top of the front legs with the fingers of your right hand, which is still supporting the chest.

e. Using the other hand, prevent the head from moving by grasping under the throat. Scratching the ears with this hand from under the throat is often very comforting.

f. Transport to the veterinarian.

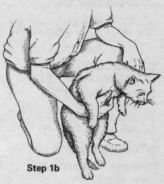

Step 1b

Steps 1c, 1d, and 1e

STEP 2: If the cat is uncooperative:

a. Drop a blanket or towel over cat.

b. Scoop the cat up so the towel or blanket encompasses the cat.

c. If you are alone, tie the ends of the towel or blanket together with cord to form a bag, or place the cat in a closed box.

d. Transport to the veterinarian.

B. IF THE CAT NEEDS A STRETCHER

STEP 1: Use a blanket or a flat board or strong piece of cardboard. If you are using a board or piece of cardboard, proceed to STEP 2.

If you are using a blanket:

a. Place one hand under the cat's chest and the other hand under its rear; carefully lift or slide the cat onto the blanket.

b. Grasp each end of the blanket and lift; keep the blanket taut to form a stretcher.

c. Transport to the veterinarian.

Step 1a

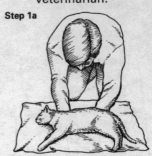

> *CAUTION: A flat board or strong piece of cardboard must be used if a broken back is suspected.*

continued

STEP 2: If you are using a flat board or strong piece of cardboard:

a. Use a firm piece of cardboard, table leaf, TV table top, cutting board, or removable bookshelf. Make sure whatever you use will fit in your car.

b. Place two or three long strips of cloth or rope under the board, avoiding the area where the cat's neck will rest.

c. Place one hand under the cat's chest and the other under its rear; carefully lift or slide the cat onto the board.

d. Tie the cat to the board to prevent it from falling.

e. Transport to the veterinarian.

Step 2c

Step 2d

Abscess

SIGNS: SOFT, PAINFUL SWELLING; FOUL-SMELLING DISCHARGE FROM OPEN WOUND; LETHARGY.

STEP 1: Clip the hair around the area.

STEP 2: If the abscess is draining, proceed to Step 3. If not, apply hot moist compresses for 20-minute periods two or three times a day until the abscess starts draining.

STEP 3: Thoroughly clean the area with 3% hydrogen peroxide two or three times a day. DO NOT use any other antiseptic. Keep a scab from forming for two or three days by picking it off with your fingernail.

STEP 4: If the cat stops eating, or the abscess does not stop draining foul-smelling material within 48 hours, or the area of involvement is very large, transport to the veterinarian as soon as possible.

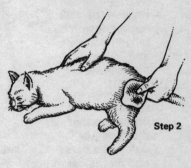

Step 2

Step 3

Administering Oral Medicine

If the cat is hard to handle, you will need help restraining it.

A. LIQUIDS

STEP 1: Restrain the cat.

a. Relieve the cat's apprehension by talking quietly and reassuringly; however, be firm.

b. Grasp the skin on the back of the neck just below the ears and lift the cat to a raised surface or table that it is unfamiliar with.

Step 1b

c. If an assistant is necessary, have him or her place both hands around the cat's shoulders and gently but firmly push the cat down on the table so it cannot use its front paws to scratch.

Step 1c

d. If the cat is somewhat aggressive, have an assistant wrap the entire cat, except the head, in a large towel.

Step 1d

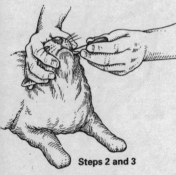

Steps 2 and 3

STEP 2: Gently hold the cat's mouth shut and tip its head up slightly.

STEP 3: Using a plastic eyedropper or dose syringe inserted into the corner of the cat's mouth, place the fluid into the mouth a little at a time, allowing each small amount to be swallowed before giving more.

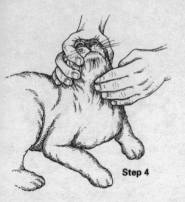

Step 4

STEP 4: Gently rub the throat to stimulate swallowing.

continued

125

B. PILLS

> *If the pill is unusually large, lubricate it with white petroleum jelly or butter.*

STEP 1: Restrain the cat.

a. Relieve the cat's apprehension by talking quietly and reassuringly; however, be firm.

Step 1b

b. Grasp the skin on the back of the neck just below the ears and lift the cat to a raised surface or table that it is unfamiliar with.

c. If an assistant is necessary, have him or her place both hands around the cat's shoulders and gently but firmly push the cat down on the table so it cannot use its front paws to scratch.

Step 1c

126

d. If the cat is somewhat aggressive, have an assistant wrap the entire cat, except the head, in a large towel.

Step 1d

STEP 2: Place one hand over the cat's head so that your thumb and index finger fall just behind the long canines (fang teeth), the head resting against your palm.

STEP 3: Gently tilt the cat's head back so its nose is pointing upward.

STEP 4: Push your thumb toward your finger; the mouth will open.

STEP 5: Hold the pill between the thumb and index finger of your other hand. Use your middle finger to push down on the lower jaw to keep it open. Place the pill as far back in the throat as possible.

STEP 6: Close the cat's mouth quickly, and gently rub its throat to stimulate swallowing.

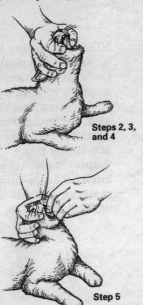

Steps 2, 3, and 4

Step 5

127

Animal Bite

STEP 1: Approach the cat (see page 112); then restrain if necessary (see page 113 or 118).

STEP 2: Clip the hair around the wound.

STEP 3: Flush thoroughly by pouring 3% hydrogen peroxide into the wound. DO NOT use any other antiseptic.

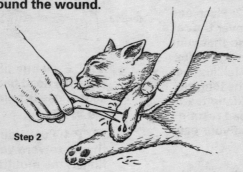

Step 2

STEP 4: Examine the wound. If the tissue under the wound appears to pass by when you move the skin, the wound will probably require stitches. If the wound is discharging a foul-smelling material, see AB-SCESS, page 123.

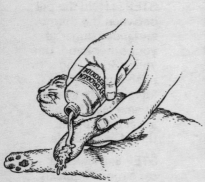

Step 3

STEP 5: DO NOT bandage. Allow the wound to drain unless there is excessive bleeding. If the wound does bleed excessively, follow these steps:

a. Cover wound with a clean cloth, sterile dressing, or sanitary napkin.

b. Place your hand over the dressing and press firmly.

c. Keep pressure on the dressing to stop bleeding. If blood soaks through the dressing, DO NOT remove.

Apply more dressing and continue to apply pressure until bleeding stops.

STEP 6: If the wound is deep enough to require stitches, transport to the veterinarian immediately.

STEP 7: If the biting animal is destroyed, take it to the veterinarian for a rabies examination. DO NOT touch it with your bare hands.

STEP 8: If the cat is not currently vaccinated for rabies, contact the veterinarian.

Steps 5a, 5b, and 5c

Bladder Infection

SIGNS: URINATING OUTSIDE THE LITTER PAN, STRAINING TO URINATE EVIDENCED BY GOING IN AND OUT OF LITTER PAN AND SQUATTING FOR LONG PERIODS OF TIME, BLOOD IN URINE, EXCESSIVE LICKING OF GENITAL AREA, VOMITING WITH ABOVE SIGNS.

A. IF THE CAT IS A MALE

STEP 1: Approach the cat (see page 112); then restrain if necessary (see page 113 or 118).

STEP 2: Check for possible obstruction of the penis, which is life-threatening.

a. Place the palm of your hand on the cat's abdomen immediately in front of the rear legs.

b. Close your fingers toward your thumb.

Step 2a

c. If the cat cries out in pain or you feel a large, firm object in the abdomen, which is the distended urinary bladder, the cat is probably obstructed; proceed to Step 3. If not, proceed to Step 6.

STEP 3: Have an assistant use one hand to apply pressure over the cat's shoulders, forcing the cat firmly down, while the assistant uses other hand to hold one or both of the back legs.

STEP 4: Lift the cat's tail to expose its hind end.

STEP 5: To provide some relief, use your fingers to gently roll the tip of the penis back and forth. This will help to dislodge crystalline obstruction. Success will be evidenced by production of urine.

STEP 6: Contact the veterinarian immediately.

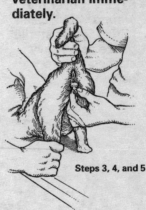

Steps 3, 4, and 5

B. IF THE CAT IS A FEMALE

STEP 1: There is no effective home treatment. Although the condition is not life-threatening, the veterinarian should be contacted.

131

BLEEDING: Spurting Blood

**WATCH FOR SIGNS OF SHOCK:
PALE OR WHITE GUMS, RAPID HEARTBEAT
AND BREATHING. IF SIGNS ARE PRESENT
SEE PAGE 187.**

A. ON HEAD OR TORSO

STEP 1: Approach
the cat (see page
112); then restrain if
necessary (see page
113 or 118).

*If any wound is
spurting blood, it
means an artery
has been cut. This
requires immediate
professional
attention.*

STEP 2: Cover the
wound with a clean,
folded towel, sterile
gauze pad, heavy
cloth, or sanitary
napkin.

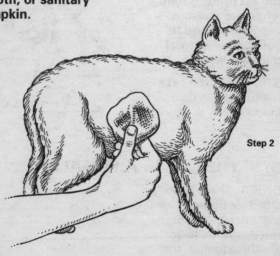

Step 2

STEP 3: Wrap torn rags or other soft material around the dressing and tie or tape just tightly enough to hold in place.

STEP 4: Transport to the veterinarian immediately.

B. ON LEGS OR TAIL

STEP 1: Approach the cat (see page 112); then restrain if necessary (see page 113 or 118).

STEP 2: Apply a tourniquet.

a. Use a tie or piece of cloth folded to about one inch width. DO NOT use rope, wire, or string.

b. Place the material between the wound and the heart, an inch or two above—but not touching—the wound.

c. Wrap the tie or cloth twice around the appendage and cross the ends.

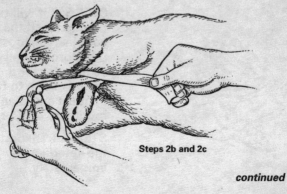

Steps 2b and 2c

continued

d. Tie a stick or ruler to the material with a single knot.

e. Twist the stick until bleeding stops, but no tighter.

f. Wrap a piece of cloth around the stick and limb to keep in place.

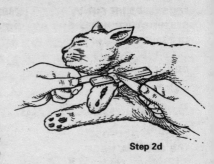

Step 2d

Step 2e

Step 2f

STEP 3: If it will take time to reach the veterinarian, loosen the tourniquet every 15 minutes for a period of one to two minutes and then retighten.

STEP 4: Transport to the veterinarian immediately.

BLEEDING: Internal

SIGNS: PALE OR WHITE GUMS; RAPID HEARTBEAT AND BREATHING; KNOWLEDGE OF INGESTION OF RAT OR MOUSE POISON; BLEEDING FROM THE EARS, NOSE, OR MOUTH WITH ANY OF THE ABOVE SIGNS.

STEP 1: If there is bleeding from any external wound, treat for shock. See page 187.

If there is no visible bleeding from any external wound, proceed to Step 2.

STEP 2: Place the cat on a blanket, towel, or jacket on its side with its head extended.

STEP 3: Clear the airway.

a. Place one hand over the cat's head so that your thumb and index finger fall just behind the long canines (fang teeth), the head resting against your palm.

b. Gently tilt the cat's head back so its nose is pointing upward. Push your thumb toward your finger; the mouth will open.

c. Gently pull out the cat's tongue to keep the airway open. If the cat resists your attempt to pull the tongue out, do not repeat Step 3.

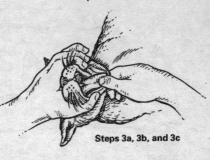

Steps 3a, 3b, and 3c

continued

STEP 4: Elevate the cat's hindquarters slightly by placing them on a pillow or folded or rolled-up towel.

STEP 5: Conserve body heat.

a. Place a hot water bottle or container (100°F/37°C) against the abdomen. Wrap the bottle in cloth to prevent burns.

b. Wrap the cat in a blanket or jacket.

STEP 6: Transport to the veterinarian immediately.

Step 4

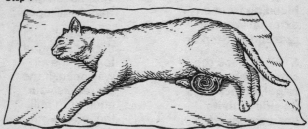

Step 5a

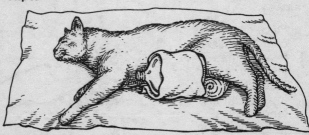

136

BLEEDING:
Chest Or Abdomen

**WATCH FOR SIGNS OF SHOCK:
PALE OR WHITE GUMS, RAPID HEARTBEAT
AND BREATHING. IF SIGNS ARE PRESENT,
SEE PAGE 187.**

STEP 1: Approach the cat (see page 112); then restrain if necessary (see page 113 or 118).

STEP 2: If the wound is in the chest and a "sucking" noise is heard, bandage tightly enough to keep air from entering and transport immediately to the veterinarian.

Step 2

continued

**STEP 3: If there is a
protruding object,
such as an arrow,
see page 183.**

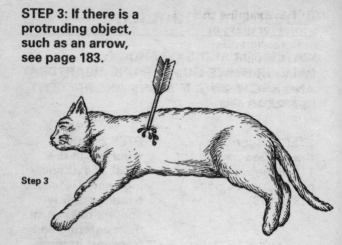

Step 3

**STEP 4: If neither of
the above situations
exists, proceed to
treat the wound:
Clip the hair around
the injured area.**

Step 4

STEP 5: Examine the wound for glass or other foreign objects. If visible, remove with fingers or tweezers. If the tissue under the wound appears to pass by when you move the skin, the wound will probably require stitches.

Step 5

STEP 6: Flush thoroughly by pouring 3% hydrogen peroxide into the wound. DO NOT use any other antiseptic.

Step 6

continued

139

STEP 7: Cover the wound with a clean cloth, sterile dressing, or sanitary napkin.

STEP 8: Place your hand over the dressing and press firmly.

STEP 9: Keep pressure on the dressing to stop bleeding. If blood soaks through the dressing, DO NOT remove. Apply more dressing and continue to apply pressure until bleeding stops.

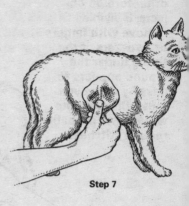

Step 7

Step 10

STEP 10: Wrap torn sheets or other soft material around the dressing and tie or tape just tightly enough to keep it in place. Transport to the veterinarian as soon as possible.

140

BLEEDING:
Leg, Paw, Or Tail

WATCH FOR SIGNS OF SHOCK: PALE OR WHITE GUMS, RAPID HEARTBEAT AND BREATHING. IF SIGNS ARE PRESENT, SEE PAGE 187.

STEP 1: Approach the cat (see page 112); then restrain if necessary (see page 113 or 118).

STEP 2: Clip the hair around the injured area.

STEP 3: Examine the wound for glass or other foreign objects. If visible, remove with fingers or tweezers. If the tissue under the wound appears to pass by when you move the skin, the wound will probably require stitches.

STEP 4: Flush thoroughly by pouring 3% hydrogen peroxide into the wound. DO NOT use any other antiseptic.

Step 2

continued

STEP 5: Cover the wound with a clean cloth, sterile dressing, or sanitary napkin.

STEP 6: Place your hand over the dressing and press firmly.

Step 3

STEP 7: Keep pressure on the dressing to stop bleeding. If blood soaks through the dressing, DO NOT remove. Apply more dressing and continue to apply pressure until bleeding stops. If bleeding does not stop within five minutes, proceed to Step 10.

Step 4

STEP 8: Wrap torn rags or other soft material around the dressing and tie or tape just tightly enough to keep it in place. Start below the wound and wrap upward.

STEP 9: If the wound is deep enough to require stitches, keep the cat off the injured leg and transport to the veterinarian immediately.

Steps 5, 6, and 7

STEP 10: If bleeding does not stop within five minutes, apply a tourniquet (see page 133).

STEP 11: If it will take time to reach the veterinarian, loosen the tourniquet every 15 minutes for a period of one to two minutes and then retighten.

Step 8

STEP 12: Transport to the veterinarian immediately.

143

BLEEDING: Nail

MOST BLEEDING NAILS ARE BROKEN AND NEED VET ATTENTION.

A. NAIL BROKEN

STEP 1: Approach the cat (see page 112); then restrain if necessary (see page 113 or 118).

STEP 2: DO NOT try to cut or remove the broken nail.

STEP 3: Unsheathe the claw.

a. Place your thumb on top of the paw, close to the nails, and your index finger on the large pad on the bottom of the paw.

b. Press your thumb and finger together. This will expose the nail for examination.

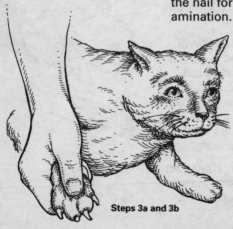

Steps 3a and 3b

STEP 4: With the nail exposed, hold a clean cloth, sterile dressing, or sanitary napkin against the nail. Bleeding will stop in a few minutes.

STEP 5: If cat seems to be in severe pain, or if bleeding does not stop in a few minutes, transport to the veterinarian as soon as possible. Continuous bleeding indicates a bleeding disorder that should be treated promptly.

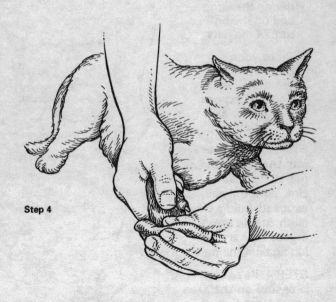

Step 4

continued

B. NAIL CUT TOO SHORT

STEP 1: Approach the cat (see page 112); then restrain if necessary (see page 113 or 118).

STEP 2: Unsheathe the claw.

a. Place your thumb on top of the paw, close to the nails, and your index finger on the large pad on the bottom of the paw.

b. Press your thumb and finger together. This will expose the nail for examination.

STEP 3: Push flour into the end of the nail to help blood clot. With the nail exposed, hold a clean cloth, sterile dressing, or sanitary napkin against the nail.

STEP 4: Keep firm pressure on the area for at least five minutes. DO NOT remove until bleeding stops.

STEP 5: If bleeding does not stop in 10 minutes, transport to the veterinarian as soon as possible. Continuous bleeding indicates a bleeding disorder that should be treated promptly.

Steps 2a and 2b

Step 3

146

BROKEN BONES:
Broken Back

SIGNS: EXTREME PAIN IN SPINE AREA, UNUSUAL ARCH TO SPINE, PARALYSIS.

WATCH FOR SIGNS OF SHOCK: PALE OR WHITE GUMS, RAPID HEARTBEAT AND BREATHING. IF SIGNS ARE PRESENT, SEE PAGE 187.

STEP 1: If you suspect a broken back, lift the cat onto a flat board without bending its back. DO NOT attempt to splint.

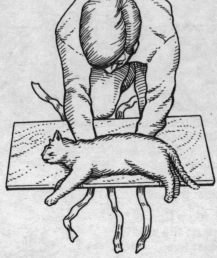

Step1c

continued

a. Use a firm piece of cardboard, table leaf, TV table top, cutting board, or removable bookshelf. Make sure whatever you use will fit in your car.

b. Place two or three long strips of cloth or rope under the board, avoiding the area where the cat's neck will rest.

c. Place one hand under the cat's chest and the other under its rear; carefully lift or slide the cat onto the board.

d. Tie the cat to the board to prevent it from falling.

STEP 2: Transport to the veterinarian immediately.

Step 1d

BROKEN BONES: Leg

SIGNS: LEG IS MISSHAPEN, HANGS LIMPLY, CANNOT SUPPORT BODY WEIGHT; SUDDEN ONSET OF PAIN IN AREA; SWELLING.

WATCH FOR SIGNS OF SHOCK: PALE OR WHITE GUMS, RAPID HEARTBEAT AND BREATHING. IF SIGNS ARE PRESENT, SEE PAGE 187.

STEP 1: Approach the cat (see page 112); then restrain if necessary (see page 113 or 118).

STEP 2: Examine the leg and determine if the fracture is open (wound near the break or bone protruding from the skin) or closed (no break in the skin).

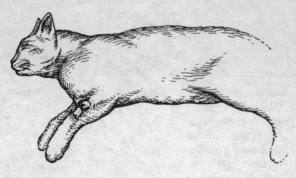

Step 2
Open Fracture

continued

STEP 3: If the fracture is closed, proceed to Step 4.

If the fracture is open:

a. Flush thoroughly by pouring 3% hydrogen peroxide into the wound. DO NOT use any other antiseptic.

Step 3a

b. Cover the wound with a clean cloth, sterile dressing, or sanitary napkin.

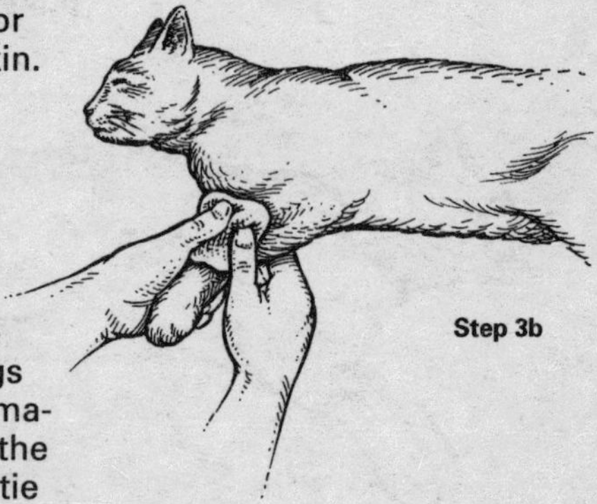

Step 3b

c. Wrap torn rags or other soft material around the dressing and tie or tape just tightly enough to keep it in place.

d. DO NOT attempt to splint the fracture. Hold a folded towel under the un-splinted limb and transport to the veterinarian immediately.

STEP 4: If the limb with the closed fracture is grossly misshapen or the cat appears to be in great pain when you attempt to splint, stop and proceed to Step 5. Otherwise, proceed to splint the bone.

Step 3d

a. Use any splint material available—sticks, a magazine, or stiff cardboard. The object is to immobilize the limb, not reset it.

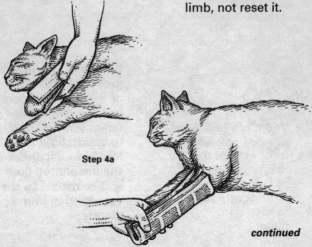

Step 4a

continued

151

b. Tie splints to the fractured leg with torn strips of cloth or gauze.

c. Tape or tie firmly, but not so tightly that circulation may be impaired.

d. Transport to the veterinarian immediately.

Steps 4b and 4c

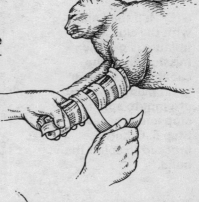

Step 5

STEP 5: If the limb is grossly misshapen, or if the cat appears to be in great pain when you attempt to splint, hold a folded towel under the unsplinted limb and transport to the veterinarian immediately.

BURNS: First Or Second Degree

SIGNS: FIRST DEGREE—FUR INTACT OR SINGED, PAINFUL LESION, SKIN RED WITH POSSIBLE BLISTERS.

SECOND DEGREE—SINGED FUR, PAINFUL LESION WHICH TURNS DRY AND TAN, SWELLING.

STEP 1: Approach the cat (see page 112); then restrain if necessary (see page 113 or 118).

STEP 2: Apply cold water or ice packs to the burned area; leave in contact with the skin for 15 minutes. DO NOT apply ointment or butter.

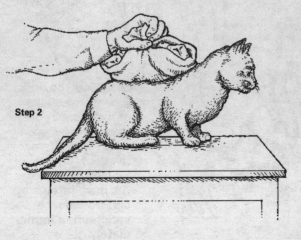

Step 2

continued

STEP 3: If burns cover a large part of the body or are located where the cat can lick them, cover with a sterile dressing. DO NOT use cotton.

STEP 4: Wrap torn rags or other soft material around the dressing and tie or tape just tightly enough to keep it in place.

STEP 5: Transport to the veterinarian as soon as possible.

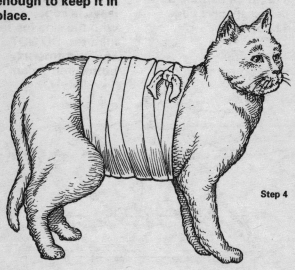

Step 4

BURNS: Third Degree

SIGNS: PROBABLE SHOCK IF EXTENSIVE BODY AREA IS INVOLVED, DESTRUCTION OF ENTIRE SKIN AREA, BLACK OR PURE WHITE LESION, FUR PULLS OUT EASILY.

WATCH FOR SIGNS OF SHOCK: PALE OR WHITE GUMS, RAPID HEARTBEAT AND BREATHING. IF SIGNS ARE PRESENT, SEE PAGE 187.

STEP 1: Approach the cat (see page 112); then restrain if necessary (see page 113 or 118).

STEP 2: Apply a sterile dressing over the burned area. DO NOT use cotton.

STEP 3: Wrap torn rags or other soft material around the dressing and tie or tape just tightly enough to keep it in place.

STEP 4: Transport to the veterinarian immediately.

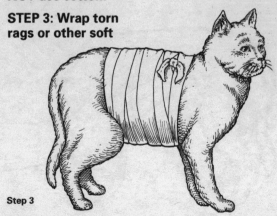

Step 3

155

BURNS: Chemical

SIGNS: CHEMICAL ODOR SUCH AS TURPENTINE, GASOLINE, OR INSECTICIDE; REDDENED SKIN; PAIN.

STEP 1: Approach the cat (see page 112); then restrain if necessary (see page 113 or 118).

STEP 2: Wearing rubber gloves, wash the area thoroughly with mild soap or shampoo and water. Lather well and rinse thoroughly. Repeat as many times as necessary to remove the chemical. DO NOT use solvents of any kind.

STEP 3: Call the veterinarian for further instructions.

Step 2

Choking

STEP 1: Approach the cat (see page 112); then restrain if necessary (see page 113 or 118).

STEP 2: Clear the airway.

a. Place one hand over the cat's head so that your thumb and index finger fall just behind the long canines (fang teeth), the head resting against your palm. If the cat is struggling too much, proceed to Step 2e.

b. Gently tilt the cat's head back so its nose is pointing upward. Push your thumb toward your finger; the mouth will open.

c. Gently pull the tongue out. If you can see the object, try to remove it with your fingers or needle-nose pliers (unless object is a needle).

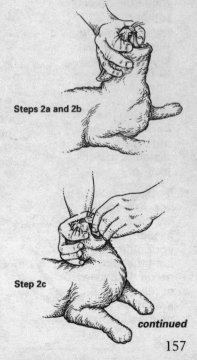

Steps 2a and 2b

Step 2c

continued

157

d. If object is a needle and it is embedded deeply into the roof of the mouth, stop. Transport immediately to the veterinarian. Keep the tongue gently pulled out of the mouth if the cat is in distress.

e. If you cannot remove the object (other than a needle), pick up the cat by grasping its back legs; turn it upside down and shake vigorously. Slapping the back while shaking may help to dislodge the object.

f. If object is still not dislodged, lay the cat on its side, place your palms behind the last rib on both sides of the abdomen, and press your palms together

quickly three or four times. If the object is still caught, repeat this procedure.

Step 2e

STEP 3: If you cannot dislodge the object, transport to the veterinarian immediately.

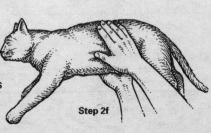

Step 2f

158

STEP 4: If you dislodge the object but the cat is not breathing, feel for heartbeat by placing fingers about one inch behind the cat's elbow and in the center of its chest.

STEP 5: If the heart is not beating, proceed to Step 6. If it is beating, perform artificial respiration.

a. Turn the cat on its side.

b. Hold the cat's mouth and lips closed and blow firmly into its nostrils. Blow for three seconds, take a deep breath, and repeat until you feel resistance or see the chest rise.

c. After one minute, stop. Watch the chest for movement to indicate the cat is breathing on its own.

d. If the cat is still not breathing, continue artificial respiration.

e. Transport to the veterinarian immediately and continue artificial respiration on the way to the veterinarian or until the cat is breathing without assistance.

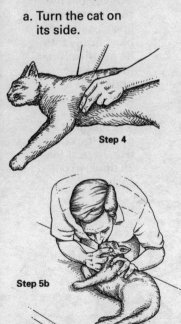

Step 4

Step 5b

continued

STEP 6: If the heart is not beating, perform CPR (cardiopulmonary resuscitation).

a. Turn the cat on its side.

b. Kneel down at the head of the cat.

c. Grasp the chest so that the breastbone is resting in the palm of your hand, your thumb on one side of the chest and your fingers on the other. Your thumb and fingers should fall in the middle of the chest.

d. Compress the chest by firmly squeezing your thumb and fingers together for a count of "two" and release for a count of "one." Repeat about 30 times in 30 seconds (one per second).

e. Alternately (after 10 compressions), hold the cat's mouth and lips closed and blow firmly into its nostrils. Blow for three seconds, take a deep breath, and repeat until you feel resistance or see the chest rise. Repeat this 20 times in 60 seconds.

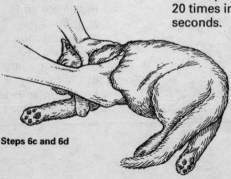

Steps 6c and 6d

f. After one minute, stop. Look at the chest for breathing movement and feel for heartbeat by placing fingers about one inch behind cat's elbow and in the center of its chest.

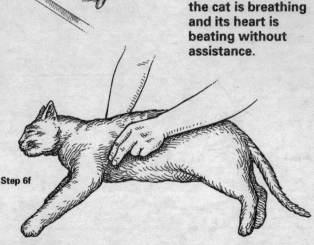

Step 6e

g. If the cat's heart is still not beating, continue CPR. If the heart starts beating, but the cat is still not breathing, return to Step 5b to continue artificial respiration.

STEP 7: Transport to the veterinarian immediately. CPR or artificial respiration should be continued on the way or until the cat is breathing and its heart is beating without assistance.

Step 6f

161

Diarrhea

STEP 1: Remove all food immediately. Water is important to prevent dehydration in severe diarrhea. It should not be removed.

STEP 2: If blood appears or if diarrhea continues for more than 24 hours, contact the veterinarian. The vet will probably want to see a stool sample.

STEP 3: Treat with Kaopectate® every four to six hours at the rate of ½ teaspoon per five to seven pounds of the cat's weight. See Administering Oral Medicine, page 124.

STEP 4: DO NOT attempt to feed for at least 12 hours.

STEP 5: After 12 hours, feed the cat a mixture of small quantities of steamed ground beef, cooked rice, and cottage cheese. If the cat rejects the ground beef, substitute boiled chicken breasts, skinned and boned. This diet should be continued until stools are formed.

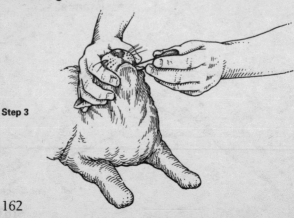

Step 3

162

Electrical Shock

**WATCH FOR SIGNS OF SHOCK:
PALE OR WHITE GUMS, RAPID HEARTBEAT
AND BREATHING. IF SIGNS ARE PRESENT,
SEE PAGE 187.**

STEP 1: If the cat
still has the electric
cord in its mouth,
DO NOT touch. First
remove the plug
from its outlet.

Step 1

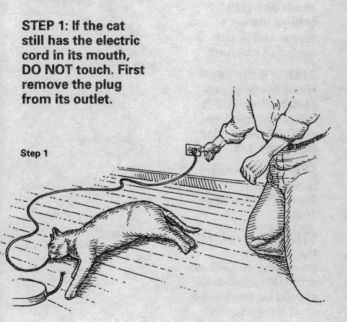

continued

Step 2

Step 3

STEP 2: If the cat is breathing, proceed to Step 6. If the cat is not breathing, feel for heartbeat by placing fingers about one inch behind the cat's elbow and in the center of its chest.

STEP 3: If the heart is not beating, proceed to Step 4. If it is beating, perform artificial respiration (see page 159).

STEP 4: If the heart is not beating, perform CPR (see page 160).

STEP 5: Transport to the veterinarian immediately. CPR or artificial respiration should be continued on the way to the veterinarian or until the cat is breathing and its heart is beating without assistance.

STEP 6: If the cat's mouth or lips are burned (bright red), swab them gently with 3% hydrogen peroxide. DO NOT use any other antiseptic.

STEP 7: Conserve body heat.

a. Move the cat onto a blanket, towel, or jacket.

b. Place a hot water bottle or container (100°F/37°C) against the cat's abdomen. Wrap the bottle in cloth to prevent burns.

c. Wrap the cat in a blanket or jacket.

STEP 8: Transport to the veterinarian immediately.

Step 6

Eye Scratch Or Irritation

SIGNS: SQUINTING, RUBBING OR PAWING AT EYES; THICK DISCHARGE; OR REDNESS.

STEP 1: Approach the cat (see page 112); then restrain if necessary (see page 113 or 118).

STEP 2: Flush thoroughly (three or four times) by pouring dilute boric acid solution or plain water into the eye.

Step 2

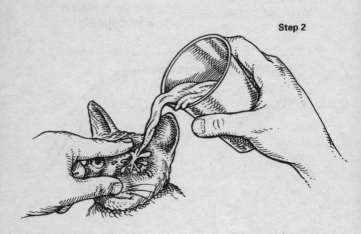

STEP 3: Prevent self-injury to the eye.

a. Dewclaw should
   be bandaged on
   the front paw on
   the same side as
   the affected eye.

Step 3a

Step 3b

b. If the cat is
   scratching at the
   eye continu-
   ously, cut a
   large piece of
   cardboard into
   an Elizabethan-
   type collar.

STEP 4: Transport to the veterinarian immediately.

167

Fall From High-Rise Building

SIGNS: BLOOD FROM NOSE AND MOUTH, BROKEN BONES, UNCONSCIOUSNESS.

WATCH FOR SIGNS OF SHOCK: PALE OR WHITE GUMS, RAPID HEARTBEAT AND BREATHING. IF SIGNS ARE PRESENT, SEE PAGE 187.

STEP 1: Look for the cat in all hiding places near where the fall took place. If cat is unconscious, see page 193.

STEP 2: Approach the cat (see page 112); then restrain if necessary (see page 113 or 118).

STEP 3: Examine for blood around the nose. If present, carefully wipe away. Bleeding should stop in a few minutes. If bleeding does not stop, transport to the veterinarian.

STEP 4: Examine for blood, broken teeth, and/or split upper palate in mouth. To open the mouth:

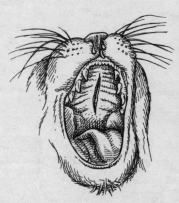

Step 4   Split Upper Palate

a. Place one hand
   over the cat's
   head so that
   your thumb and
   index finger fall
   just behind the
   long canines
   (fang teeth), the
   head resting
   against your
   palm.

b. Gently tilt the
   cat's head back
   so its nose is
   pointing up-
   ward. Push your
   thumb toward
   your finger; the
   mouth will open.

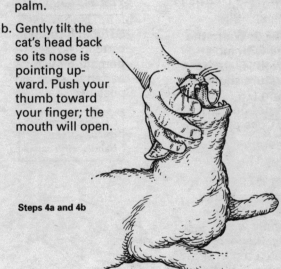

Steps 4a and 4b

**STEP 5: Carefully
wipe blood away
from mouth; bleed-
ing should stop in a
few minutes.**

**STEP 6: Examine for
broken bones. See
pages 147–152.**

**STEP 7: Transport to
the veterinarian
immediately.**

169

Frostbite

SIGNS: PAIN, PALE SKIN IN EARLY STAGES, RED OR BLACK SKIN IN ADVANCED STAGES.

STEP 1: Approach the cat (see page 112); then restrain if necessary (see page 113 or 118).

The most commonly affected areas are the ears, tail, and feet.

STEP 2: Warm the area with moist towels. Water temperature should be warm (75°F/24°C), but not hot. DO NOT use ointment.

STEP 3: If the skin turns dark, transport to the veterinarian as soon as possible.

Caution: Frostbite can be painful. Handle wiith care.

Step 2

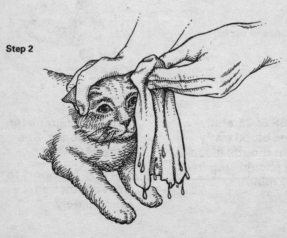

170

Hairball

SIGNS: CAT VOMITS UP LONG CIGAR-SHAPED MATERIAL FULL OF HAIR; VOMITS FOOD IMMEDIATELY AFTER EATING AND ATTEMPTS TO EAT AGAIN; PASSES HAIR IN STOOL; RARELY, LACK OF APPETITE AND WEIGHT LOSS.

STEP 1: Remove all food and water immediately.

STEP 2: If vomited material is bloody or has a foul odor, contact the veterinarian immediately. If not, proceed to Step 3.

STEP 3: Treat by placing one or two teaspoons of white petroleum jelly on the cat's mouth and paws so it can lick it off. DO NOT give mineral oil.

STEP 4: Repeat the petroleum jelly treatment once a day while the cat is having difficulty. If problem lasts more than two or three days, contact the veterinarian as soon as possible.

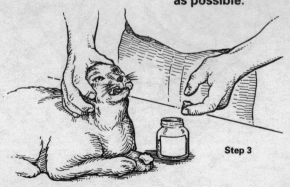

Step 3

Heart Disease

SIGNS: DIFFICULT BREATHING, LACK OF COORDINATION OR PARALYSIS OF REAR LIMBS, EXCESSIVE CRYING WITH ABOVE SIGNS.

STEP 1: Carefully wrap the cat in a blanket or towel so it feels secure.

STEP 2: There is no effective home treatment. The situation is life-threatening, and the cat should be taken to the veterinarian immediately.

Step 1

Heatstroke

SIGNS: EXCESSIVE DROOLING, LACK OF COORDINATION, RAPID BREATHING, TOP OF THE HEAD HOT TO THE TOUCH.

STEP 1: Remove the cat from the hot environment.

Prompt treatment is urgent. Heatstroke can lead to brain damage and death.

STEP 2: Immerse the cat in a cold water bath or continuously run a garden hose on its body; continue either treatment for at least 30 minutes.

Step 2

Step 3

STEP 3: Apply ice packs around the head; keep them there while transporting to the veterinarian.

STEP 4: Transport to the veterinarian immediately after the above treatment.

173

POISONING: Corrosive Or Petroleum-Base

SIGNS: BURNS ON MOUTH IF CORROSIVE, CHARACTERISTIC ODOR IF PETROLEUM PRODUCT, SEVERE ABDOMINAL PAIN, VOMITING, DIARRHEA, BLOODY URINE, CONVULSIONS, COMA.

WATCH FOR SIGNS OF SHOCK: PALE OR WHITE GUMS, RAPID HEARTBEAT AND BREATHING. IF SIGNS ARE PRESENT, SEE PAGE 187.

Corrosives include battery acid, corn and callous remover, dishwasher detergent, drain cleaner, grease remover, lye, and oven cleaner. Petroleum products include paint solvent, floor wax, and dry cleaning solution. If in doubt as to type of poison, call your veterinarian or local Poison Control Center.

STEP 1: If the cat is comatose or convulsing, wrap it in a blanket and take the cat and container of suspected poison to the veterinarian immediately. If not, proceed to Step 2.

STEP 2: Approach the cat (see page 112); then restrain if necessary (see page 113 or 118).

STEP 3: Flush the cat's mouth and muzzle thoroughly with large amounts of water. Hold its head at a slight downward angle so it does not choke.

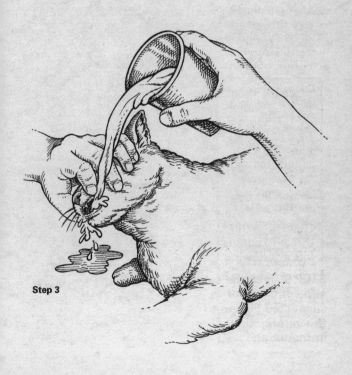

Step 3

continued

STEP 4: DO NOT induce vomiting. Give one teaspoon of olive oil or egg whites.

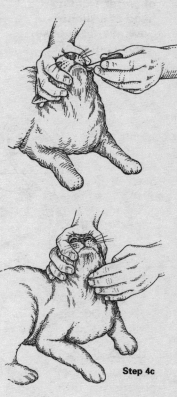

Steps 4a and 4b

a. Gently hold the cat's mouth shut and tip its head up slightly.

b. Using a plastic eye-dropper or dose syringe inserted into the corner of the cat's mouth, place the fluid into the corner of the mouth a little at a time, allowing each small amount to be swallowed before giving more.

c. Gently rub the throat to stimulate swallowing.

Step 4c

STEP 5: Take the cat and container of suspected poison to the veterinarian immediately.

POISONING: Noncorrosive

SIGNS: EXCESSIVE DROOLING, VOMITING, ABDOMINAL PAIN, LACK OF COORDINATION, CONVULSIONS, COMA.

WATCH FOR SIGNS OF SHOCK: PALE OR WHITE GUMS, RAPID HEARTBEAT AND BREATHING. IF SIGNS ARE PRESENT, SEE PAGE 187.

STEP 1: If the cat is comatose or convulsing, wrap it in a blanket and take the cat and container of suspected poison to the veterinarian immediately.

STEP 2: Approach the cat (see page 112); then restrain if necessary (see page 113 or 118).

STEP 3: If the cat has not already vomited, induce vomiting immediately by giving one teaspoon of 3% hydrogen peroxide every 10 minutes until the cat vomits.

a. Gently hold the cat's mouth shut and tip its head up slightly.

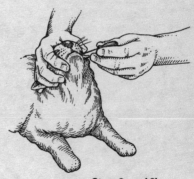

Steps 3a and 3b

continued

177

b. Using a plastic eye-dropper or dose syringe inserted into the corner of the cat's mouth, place the fluid into the corner of the mouth a little at a time, allowing each small amount to be swallowed before giving more.

c. Gently rub the throat to stimulate swallowing.

STEP 4: Save the vomit for the veterinarian.

STEP 5: Take the cat, vomit, and container of suspected poison to the veterinarian immediately.

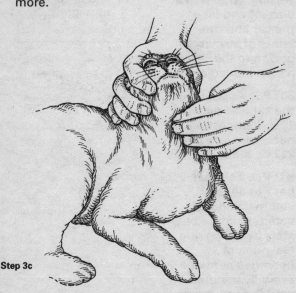

Step 3c

POISONING:
Poisonous Plants

SIGNS: DROOLING, VOMITING, DIARRHEA, ABDOMINAL PAIN, LACK OF COORDINATION, DIFFICULTY IN BREATHING, CONVULSIONS.

STEP 1: Approach the cat (see page 112); then restrain if necessary (see page 113 or 118).

STEP 2: If the cat has not vomited, induce vomiting by giving one teaspoon of 3% hydrogen peroxide every 10 minutes until the cat vomits

> *See list of toxic plants on page 48. It is safe to assume that all common houseplants are toxic to some degree.*

a. Gently hold the cat's mouth shut and tip its head up slightly.

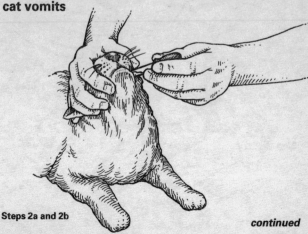

Steps 2a and 2b

continued

b. Using a plastic eye-dropper or dose syringe inserted into the corner of the cat's mouth, place the fluid into the corner of the mouth a little at a time, allowing each small amount to be swallowed before giving more.

c. Gently rub the throat to stimulate swallowing.

STEP 3: If convulsions or difficulty in breathing develops, take the cat and a leaf of the suspected plant to the veterinarian immediately. If vomiting continues, transport to the vet.

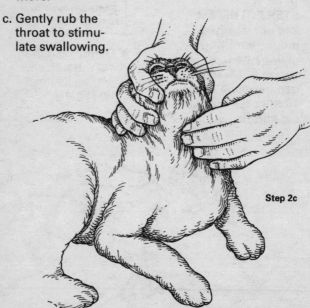

Step 2c

POISONING: Smoke Or Carbon Monoxide Inhalation

SIGNS: DEPRESSION, LACK OF COORDINATION, HEAVY PANTING, DEEP RED GUMS, POSSIBLE CONVULSIONS.

WATCH FOR SIGNS OF SHOCK: PALE OR WHITE GUMS, RAPID HEARTBEAT AND BREATHING. IF SIGNS ARE PRESENT, SEE PAGE 187.

A. IF CONSCIOUS

STEP 1: Remove the cat to fresh air immediately.

STEP 2: Flush the cat's eyes thoroughly by pouring dilute boric acid solution or plain water directly into them.

STEP 3: Transport to the veterinarian immediately.

Step 2

continued

B. IF UNCONSCIOUS

STEP 1: Remove the cat to fresh air immediately.

STEP 2: If the cat is not breathing, feel for heartbeat by placing fingers about one inch behind the cat's elbow and in the center of its chest.

STEP 3: If the heart is not beating, proceed to Step 4. If it is beating, perform artificial respiration (see page 159).

STEP 4: If the heart is not beating, perform CPR (see page 160).

STEP 5: Transport to the veterinarian immediately. CPR or artificial respiration should be continued on the way to the veterinarian or until the cat is breathing and its heart is beating without assistance.

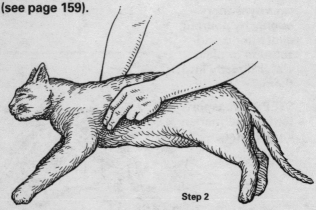

Step 2

Puncture Wound

SIGNS: BLOOD-TINGED FUR, LIMPING.

**WATCH FOR SIGNS OF SHOCK:
PALE OR WHITE GUMS, RAPID HEARTBEAT
AND BREATHING. IF SIGNS ARE PRESENT,
SEE PAGE 187.**

A. IF OBJECT (KNIFE, ARROW, STICK, ETC.) IS PROTRUDING

STEP 1: Approach the cat (see page 112); then restrain if necessary (see page 113 or 118). Take care not to touch the object.

STEP 2: DO NOT attempt to remove the object.

STEP 3: Place clean cloths, sterile dressings, or sanitary napkins around the point of entry.

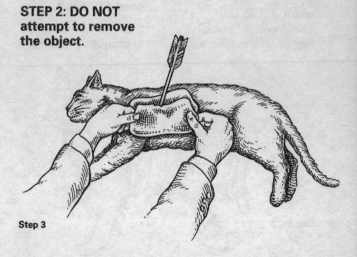

Step 3

continued

STEP 4: If the wound is in the chest, bandage tightly around the point of entry.

STEP 5: Transport immediately to the veterinarian.

Step 4

B. OTHER PUNCTURE WOUNDS

STEP 1: Approach the cat (see page 112); then restrain if necessary (see page 113 or 118).

STEP 2: If the wound is in the chest and a "sucking" noise is heard, bandage tightly enough to keep air from entering and transport immediately to the veterinarian. If not, proceed to Step 3.

STEP 3: Clip the hair around the wound.

Step 2

184

STEP 4: Examine the wound carefully for foreign objects such as glass or wood splinters. If present, remove with tweezers or needle-nose pliers.

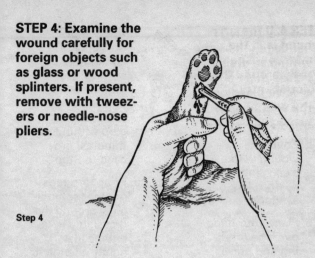

Step 4

STEP 5: Flush thoroughly by pouring 3% hydrogen peroxide into the wound. DO NOT use any other antiseptic.

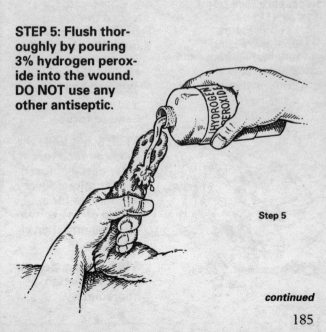

Step 5

continued

185

STEP 6: DO NOT bandage. Allow the wound to drain unless there is excessive bleeding. If the wound does bleed excessively:

a. Cover the wound with a clean cloth, sterile dressing, or sanitary napkin.

b. Place your hand over the dressing and press firmly.

c. Keep pressure on the dressing to stop bleeding. If blood soaks through the dressing, DO NOT remove.

Apply more dressing and continue to apply pressure until bleeding stops. If bleeding does not stop within five minutes, proceed to Step 7.

d. Wrap torn rags or other soft material around the dressing and tie or tape just tightly enough to keep it in place.

STEP 7: If bleeding does not stop within five minutes, apply a tourniquet (see page 133). DO NOT apply a tourniquet to the head or torso.

STEP 8: If it will take time to reach the veterinarian, loosen the tourniquet every 15 minutes for a period of one to two minutes and then retighten.

STEP 9: Transport to the veterinarian immediately.

Step 6d

Shock

SIGNS: PALE OR WHITE GUMS, VERY FAST HEARTBEAT (OVER 150 BEATS PER MINUTE), RAPID BREATHING.

STEP 1: Examine for shock.

a. Examine the gums by gently lifting the upper lip so the gum is visible. Pale or white gums indicate the cat is almost certainly in shock and may have serious internal injuries and/or bleeding. If the gums are pink, the cat is probably not in shock.

b. Determine the heartbeat. Place your fingers firmly on the cat's chest about one inch behind the cat's elbow and in the center of its chest. If the cat is in shock, its heartbeat may be well more than 150 beats per minute.

> *Any trauma or serious injury can cause shock. If the cat is in shock, do not take time to splint fractures or treat minor injuries.*

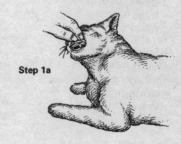

Step 1a

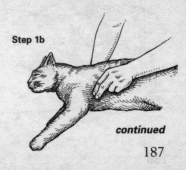

Step 1b

continued

187

STEP 2: Place the cat on a blanket, towel, or jacket on its side with its head extended.

STEP 3: Clear the airway.

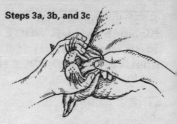

Steps 3a, 3b, and 3c

a. Place one hand over the cat's head so that your thumb and index finger fall just behind the long canines (fang teeth), the head resting against your palm.

b. Gently tilt the cat's head back so its nose is pointing upward. Push your thumb toward

your finger; the mouth will open.

c. Gently pull out the cat's tongue to keep the airway open. If the cat resists your attempt to pull the tongue out, do not repeat Step 3.

STEP 4: Elevate the cat's hindquarters slightly by placing them on a pillow or folded or rolled-up towel.

Step 4

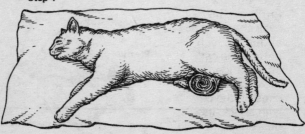

STEP 5: Stop visible bleeding immediately; if blood is spurting and the wound is on a leg or the tail, proceed to Step 6. If there is no visible bleeding, proceed to Step 8.

a. Cover the wound with a clean cloth, sterile dressing, or sanitary napkin.

b. Place your hand over the dressing and press firmly.

c. Keep pressure on the dressing to stop bleeding. If blood soaks through the dressing, DO NOT remove. Apply more dressing and continue to apply pressure until bleeding stops. If bleeding does not stop within five minutes, proceed to Step 6.

d. Wrap rags or other soft material around the dressing and tie or tape just tightly enough to keep it in place.

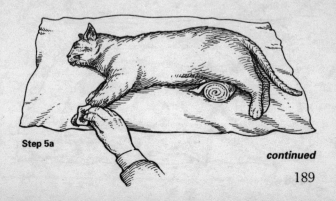

Step 5a

continued

STEP 6: Apply a tourniquet (see page 133).

STEP 7: If it will take time to reach the veterinarian, loosen the tourniquet every 15 minutes for a period of one or two minutes and then retighten.

STEP 8: Conserve body heat.

a. Place a hot water bottle or container (100°F/37°C) against the cat's abdomen. Wrap the bottle in cloth to prevent burns.

b. Wrap the cat in a blanket or jacket.

STEP 9: Transport to the veterinarian immediately.

Step 8a

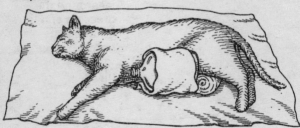

Step 8b

Swallowing Thread, String, Or Yarn

SIGNS: THREAD, STRING, OR YARN HANGING OUT OF THE MOUTH OR RECTUM; VOMITING COMBINED WITH HISTORY OF PLAYING WITH THREAD, STRING, OR YARN; LOSS OF APPETITE WITH ABOVE SIGNS.

STEP 1: Approach the cat (see page 112); then restrain if necessary (see page 113 or 118).

STEP 2: If nothing is visible, proceed to Step 3. If thread, string, or yarn is hanging out of the cat's mouth or rectum:

a. Pull lightly. If you feel resistance, stop. DO NOT continue to pull.

b. Cut off as short as possible and then proceed to Step 3.

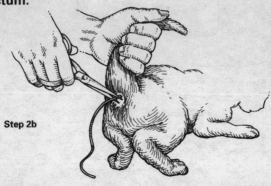

Step 2b

continued

STEP 3: Give the cat one tablespoon of white petroleum jelly. Using a small amount each time, rub the jelly on the cat's mouth and paws. The cat will lick it off. **DO NOT give mineral oil.**

STEP 4: If vomiting occurs or the cat stops eating, transport to the veterinarian immediately.

Step 3

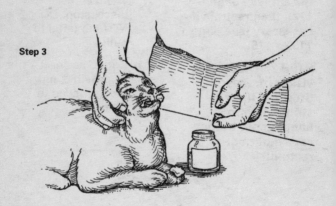

Unconsciousness

STEP 1: If you suspect choking, see page 157.

STEP 2: If the cat is breathing, check for shock. See page 187. If the cat is not breathing, proceed to Step 3.

STEP 3: Feel for heartbeat by placing fingers about one inch behind the cat's elbow and in the center of its chest.

STEP 4: If the heart is not beating, proceed to Step 5. If it is beating, perform artificial respiration (see page 159).

STEP 5: If the heart is not beating, perform CPR (see page 160).

STEP 6: Transport to the veterinarian immediately. CPR or artificial respiration should be continued on the way to the veterinarian or until the cat is breathing and its heart is beating without assistance.

Step 3

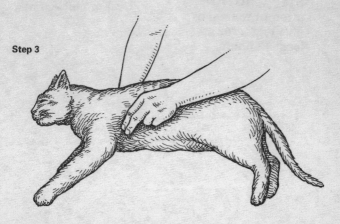

Vomiting

STEP 1: Remove all food and water immediately.

STEP 2: If vomiting contains blood or is frequent, contact the veterinarian immediately. If not, proceed to Step 3.

STEP 3: Treat with Pepto-Bismol® every four hours at the rate of ½ teaspoons per five to seven pounds of the cat's weight. See Administering Oral Medicine, page 124.

STEP 4: DO NOT attempt to feed or give water for at least 12 hours.

STEP 5: After 12 hours, feed the cat a mixture of small quantities of steamed ground beef, cooked rice, and cottage cheese. If the cat rejects the ground beef, substitute boiled chicken breasts, skinned and boned. If this is held down, a transition to regular diet should take place over the next two days by mixing an increasing quantity of regular cat food with the ground beef or chicken mix.

The Whys Of Emergency Treatment

Approaching An Injured Cat

To successfully help an injured cat, you must remember it has five weapons—the mouth and four sets of claws. It is discouraging to be scratched or bitten by a frightened pet you are trying to assist. But because it is frightened, it will either run or, if cornered, attack.

Therefore, when approaching an injured cat, move slowly and talk reassuringly. Stoop down to the cat's level so it feels more comfortable with your presence. Watch the eyes and body language to see the cat's reaction to you. If the cat is shivering and crouching, you can attempt to pet it for reassurance. Pet the cat behind the head first. If it lets you pet it in this area, then pet the rest of the head and neck area.

Scratching the ears and stroking under the chin are very comforting to a cat; it will often push its head up into your hand for more of this attention. However, if the cat is hissing, growling, and striking out with its paws, it may be very difficult to handle. Some cats react this way for only a short time to test your patience. It is a good idea to continue to talk to the cat for a few minutes to see if it will calm down enough for you to be able to restrain it.

Restraining An Injured Cat

Once you have approached the cat and determined if it is cooperative or uncooperative, the next step is to choose the method of restraint that will best fit the circumstances. Your choice will depend upon the availability of an assistant, the type and location of the cat's injury, and the first aid treatment necessary.

Restraining a cooperative cat means keeping it still so that treatment can be administered properly. The lifting procedure is easy as long as you avoid fumbling and use quick, decisive movements. Some cats prefer to be held in your arms during treatment; others will need to be restrained on a table. When restraining on a table, try to select a surface with which the cat is unfamiliar. This puts the cat in a precarious situation, which may help keep it cautious and subdued.

When the cat is uncooperative, the restraint is used not only to quiet the cat so that first aid can be administered, but also to protect you from injury. Again, the cat's weapons are its mouth and claws.

The best way to handle an uncooperative cat is to drop a blanket or towel over it and scoop it up quickly. Be sure all four paws are inside the cover. Then, the injured portion of the body can be exposed for treatment, or the cat can be transported to the veterinarian.

Some cats are impossible to handle when injured. In this case, drop the blanket or towel over the cat and gather the edges together to form a bag. As a rule, a cat feels secure covered or in a box. It may struggle a little, but you are protected. Once at the veterinarian's office, he or she can tranquilize the cat before treatment.

Transporting An Injured Cat

The injured cat can be transported to the veterinarian either held in your arms or placed in a cardboard box or cat carrier. If you suspect a broken back, try not to move the cat more than necessary to avoid further injury to the spinal cord. Tie the cat gently onto a stiff board to prevent movement while being transported to the veterinarian, and have someone call ahead to be certain he or she is prepared for your arrival.

Abscess

An abscess is a localized infection filled with pus. The body creates walls around these wounds and the pus collects within the walls.

Abscesses in cats are usually caused by bite wounds or scratches, and may be multiple when they occur. The infection results from bacteria carried on the teeth or claws of the attacking animal, which enters the skin through the bite or scratch. Most abscesses will be located around the neck, front legs, or the tail and rump area. Many times owners fail to realize the cat has been bitten until they find a soft, painful swelling on the body or a foul-smelling discharge on the fur.

Fur should be clipped from the suspected area to make cleaning easier and also to aid in drainage of the wound. The area should then be flushed thoroughly with 3% hydrogen peroxide if the abscess is open. If the abscess has not yet broken open, hot compresses should be applied for 20 minutes two or three times per day until it opens and starts draining. Never try to cut an abscess open yourself to establish drainage. This should be left to a veterinarian. The cat may lick the abscess in an attempt to open it if the affected area is within its reach. When it does open, 3% hydrogen peroxide should be used liberally to help kill the bacteria. If the abscess is discovered too late, there may be extensive damage to the muscles and other tissues under the skin. This requires professional attention as soon as possible. It is advisable to keep a draining abscess open for two or three days by picking the scab off. This will prevent buildup of the pus and speed healing.

Animal Bite

If your cat has been in a fight, examine it for hidden wounds. You'll often find punctures around the neck area, rump area, and on the legs. Look through the hair to find blood stains, which would indicate the skin has been punctured.

After clipping the hair from around the wound to assess the damage, flush with 3% hydrogen peroxide to prevent infection. This is one of the major complications of a bite.

Although there may be only a few punctures, extensive damage may have been done to underlying muscles. If the wounds are deep enough to require stitches, this should be done as soon as possible by a professional.

198

Unless there is extensive bleeding, the wounds should be left open to drain until the cat is seen by the veterinarian. Whenever tissue is damaged, fluid accumulates in the area. If the wound is not left open to drain, a painful swelling will occur and the site will become a perfect medium for the growth of bacteria and infection.

If possible, it is important to determine if the biting animal has been inoculated against rabies. If the biting animal is a wild animal such as a skunk or raccoon, efforts should be made to destroy it so the brain can be examined for rabies. Never touch the animal with your bare hands, even after it has been killed. Wear gloves or wrap the body in a blanket. Your veterinarian will take care of the rabies examination.

Bladder Infection

An area of concern to cat owners and veterinarians is bladder infections, medically known as Feline Urological Syndrome or cystitis. This disease is not limited to male cats but is of great danger to them because of their anatomy. The male cat has an extremely small tube (urethra) leading from the bladder through the penis. In most cases, cystitis causes the formation of a crystalline substance in the urine, which will clog the urethra of male cats and make urination impossible. This will be evidenced by the cat straining in the litter pan as if constipated and producing only small drops of urine, crying while straining, squatting outside the litter pan, and licking its genital area frequently. If the cat is plugged and cannot urinate, the kidneys will lose the ability to remove the waste products from the blood. This causes a buildup of nitrogen by-products in the blood known as uremia, which can lead to death. A blocked male cat that is vomiting is probably uremic and will die if not treated immediately. Call your veterinarian, regardless of the time of day or night.

Female cats also get cystitis, and though the symptoms are the same as those of a male, females will not plug up, and the midnight emergency does not exist.

In all cases of cystitis, diet changes are recommended. Most urinary stones and urethral plugs are made up of struvite crystals. These crystals are made up of magnesium ammonium phosphate hexahydrate. Diet influences the precipitation of these crystals by altering the urinary pH (acidity). As urine becomes more acidic, less struvite will precipitate. When a diet containing excess magnesium is consumed, struvite crystals will develop.

It is recommended that diets should contain fewer than 20 mg magnesium/100 kcal and maintain a urinary pH of between 6.0 and 6.4. Many food manufacturers have changed their diets to comply with these recommendations. As a result, fewer struvite crystals are being seen and more oxalate crystals are being diagnosed. In order to prevent the formation of oxalate stones, a diet that produces an alkaline urine is required. It is important that any cat with cystitis be on the correct diet as determined by your veterinarian. Several surgical procedures have been developed to help prevent obstruction in the male. While these procedures are very successful, the cat can still have uncomfortable attacks of cystitis.

Bleeding

With a bleeding injury, the main purpose of first aid is to prevent excessive blood loss that can lead to shock. Pressure applied to the wound allows the normal clotting mechanism of the blood to stop the leak. This is a complex process, but basically the blood cells form a fine screen over the wound and thus prevent further loss of blood. That is why it is important not to remove the dressing once it has been applied. If you lift it to look at the wound, it will break up the clots that are forming and the wound will continue to bleed.

If the wound continues to bleed through the dressing, it will be necessary to use a tourniquet. The tourniquet should be used only as a last resort, because although it stops the bleeding, it also prevents blood from getting to other tissues in the area, which become oxygen starved and die.

Blood is carried from the heart by the arteries and returned by the veins. If an artery is cut, the blood will spurt with each beat of the heart. Cut arteries require immediate care to stop the bleeding and usually require veterinary care for repair.

Internal bleeding can be caused by a ruptured liver or spleen as the result of an accident, or the ingestion of an anticoagulant such as rat or mouse poison. Symptoms are pale or white gums; rapid heartbeat and breathing; availability of rat or mouse poison; and bleeding from the ears, nose, or mouth with any of the above signs. Shock almost always follows. Therefore, the cat's tongue should be gently pulled forward to keep the airway open, and the hindquarters should be elevated slightly. It is important to conserve body heat by placing a wrapped hot water bottle against the abdomen and wrapping the cat in a blanket or jacket. Since shock is often fatal, transport the cat to the veterinarian immediately.

Cats love to keep their nails sharp. Often, their nails will break during a fight or because they are too long. There is a blood vessel and nerve in the center of each nail. This is seen as the pink area in white nails. If you cut your cat's nails yourself, it is important not to cut into the "quick," as it is called, but to clip the nail just in front of it. If the "quick" is cut, the nail will bleed and the cut nerve will cause some pain. If your cat is nervous or upset, have a professional cut its nails.

Broken Bones

With cats, as with human beings, all bones are subject to breakage, but leg fractures are by far the most common. It is important to remember that cats have a high pain tolerance, and often a dangling leg seems to cause no pain. Therefore, don't be afraid to handle the fractured limb (gently!). The cat will let you know if it hurts. If the cat is in pain or if the fracture is open, do not attempt to splint. An open fracture is one in which the bone protrudes or there is a break in the skin over the broken bone. First aid efforts should be directed to the control of infection, since the exposed bone is subject to bacterial invasion. Proper cleaning is of prime importance. Use only 3% hydrogen peroxide, as other antiseptics may cause tissue damage. Then, hold a large towel under the limb for support and transport the cat to the veterinarian.

A closed fracture is one with the bone broken but the skin intact. The leg should be splinted, but do not confuse splinting with setting the limb. The limb should be set by a professional. Splinting is only a temporary procedure, so you may use any firm material at hand. The purpose of a splint is to prevent further damage by immobilizing the limb and to make the animal more comfortable during the trip.

In severe accidents, spinal or rib fractures can occur. If the cat is paralyzed, or if there is an unusual arch to the back, the back may be broken. To prevent further damage to the spinal cord, it is very important that you do not move the cat more than necessary. The spinal cord lies inside the bony vertebrae of the back. If these vertebrae are bent while moving the cat, more severe damage can occur to the irreparable spinal cord. It is for this reason that the utmost care must be taken while sliding the cat onto a flat board for transportation.

Broken ribs are not quite as frequent in cats as in dogs. When they do occur, it is important to take care in handling the cat. Occasionally, a fractured rib will enter the thorax (chest cavity) and the sharp bone can puncture a lung or even the heart. If the cat can be handled, bandage the chest to prevent further damage. However, if the cat is uncontrollable, do not attempt bandaging. Simply wrap it in a blanket and transport it to the vet.

Burns

Burns can be caused by fire, heat, boiling liquids, chemicals, and electricity. All are painful and can cause damage, even death. Most scalds can be avoided by care in the kitchen. Because the cat is often on countertops or underfoot while its owner is cooking, care should be taken when handling hot water or cooking oil.

Superficial burns, evidenced by pain and reddening of the skin, are usually not serious. However, first aid should be given as soon as possible to ease the pain. Burns tend to "cook" the skin, and cold water or ice packs should be applied at once to the burned area.

At one time, the recommended treatment was the application of butter or grease, until it was discovered that these products could actually make the wound worse. They should never be used.

Third degree burns are far more serious. Depending on how much of the body is involved, they can cause death. The deeper the layers of skin involved, the more likely the cat is to go into shock. The outer skin layers are destroyed, and the unprotected lower layers are then susceptible to infection. If the burns are extensive, a great deal of fluid from the tissue cells will be lost and shock is certain to result. Treatment for shock is your first priority and should be continued until professional help can be obtained.

In burns due to fire, the airway and lungs may also be seriously damaged by inhalation of smoke and heated air. Burned lungs collect fluid, causing shortness of breath. To ease breathing, the cat's head should be kept higher than its body. Also, a burned airway may swell shut; it is imperative to keep this airway open. Immediate professional help is essential.

Chemical burns can also endanger our pets. Products such as drain cleaners or paint thinners can cause serious skin damage, and poisoning if swallowed. To prevent accidents of this nature, these products should be kept out of the cat's reach.

If you notice a chemical odor on your cat, often the first sign of this type of burn, bathe it immediately. Do not use solvents of any kind on the skin. Use mild soap, lather well, and then rinse thoroughly until the odor has disappeared. After bathing, veterinary care will be necessary.

Choking

When a cat is choking on a foreign object, it needs help at once. The harder it tries to breathe, the more panicky it becomes. Your goal is to open the airway without being bitten. If you cannot reach the object with your fingers or needle-nose pliers, or if the cat is struggling too much, turn it upside down and shake it. This will often dislodge the object and propel it out of the mouth.

Another method that may be used is similar to the Heimlich maneuver in humans. Sudden thrusts on the abdomen just behind the ribcage cause the diaphragm to bulge forward into the chest. This, in turn, forces air, and frequently the object, out of the windpipe.

If the animal is unconscious and you believe a foreign object is present, you must open the airway before giving artificial respiration or cardiac massage. If the cat cannot breathe, efforts to revive it will be fruitless.

The method of artificial respiration presented in this book is the most effective. Blowing directly into the cat's nostrils fully inflates the lungs and the result is maximum oxygenation of the blood.

Cardiac massage keeps the blood pumping through the vessels and stimulates the heart muscle to contract and start beating again. With cats, you compress the heart by actually squeezing it between your thumb and fingers. This helps keep the blood pressure up and hopefully will start normal heart muscle contractions. If the brain becomes blood starved and receives no oxygen, death will follow. If you are in doubt about how long you should continue CPR, keep doing it until you see the cat breathing by itself or until you can get to a veterinarian. You can never overdo CPR, and continued efforts may actually save a life.

Diarrhea

Diarrhea is a commonly encountered problem that occurs when food is passed through the intestine too rapidly. It can be caused by allergies, milk, worms, spoiled food, or plants. There are also more serious causes such as tumors, viral infections, and diseases of the liver, pancreas, and kidney.

Initial treatment at home should be conservative, with a diet that is bland, easily digested, and binding. Follow the steps on page 162. However, it is important to seek professional help if signs of blood, severe depression, or abdominal pain are present.

Electrical Shock

Grown cats are seldom victims of electrical shock. But kittens are naturally curious and will chew almost anything, including electric cords. If the insulation is punctured and the mouth comes in contact with both wires, the cat will receive a shock and may be unable to release the cord.

You must disconnect the cord from the socket immediately, before touching the cat. If you touch the cat before disconnecting the cord, you can also be electrocuted.

Once the cord is disconnected, you can safely touch the cat. Examine it carefully. Electrocution can cause severe heart damage and fluid accumulation in the lungs. Strong shock can stop the heart, and cardiopulmonary resuscitation (CPR) must be performed immediately to start the heart beating.

Often, the mouth will be burned from contact with the bare wires. This looks much more serious than it is and will heal eventually if cleaned and treated properly.

Most electrical shocks require professional attention; the cat should be taken to the veterinarian as soon as possible.

Eye Scratch Or Irritation

Irritations to the eye can be caused by viruses, allergies, dust and dirt, fights, etc. An irritation can result in a mild inflammation of the tissue around the eye (conjunctivitis) or severe damage to the cornea. Upper respiratory diseases are probably the most common cause of conjunctivitis in cats.

When examining the eye, it is important to know that cats have a third eyelid located in the corner of the eye nearest the nose. This third eyelid can completely cover the eyeball and sometimes gives the appearance that part of the eye is gone. If it is raised and looks red, the eye is inflamed. Do not touch or manipulate this eyelid.

Other indications that the eye is irritated are squinting and rubbing or pawing at the eye. Your first priority is to prevent self-injury; this often causes more serious damage than the original irritation. Bandaging the dewclaw on the front paw of the affected side will help to prevent further damage from scratching. Placing a large piece of cardboard, shaped into an Elizabethan-type collar, around the cat's neck will prevent any scratching. All eye irritations should be treated by a vet.

Fall From High-Rise Building

This problem is often referred to as High-Rise Syndrome. Apartment cats frequently sit in a window and gaze at the birds as they fly by, or try to catch insects that land on the window sills. Unfortunately, not all windows are protected by sturdy screens, and occasionally the mesmerized cat springs at the bird or insect, and down it goes.

A cat usually survives a fall of up to five stories without serious injury. In a fall from a greater height, the tendency to land on all four feet usually holds true and leg fractures are common. As the cat hits the ground, the head is thrust downward and the chin hits first. This usually breaks teeth and splits the upper palate, which causes the nose to bleed. Shock and internal injuries occur. Cat owners in high-rises should make sure their windows have securely fastened screens. A fallen cat should be transported to the vet.

Frostbite

When a cat is exposed to freezing temperatures for a long period of time, there is always the possibility of frostbite. The areas most likely to be frostbitten are the extremities (ears, tail, feet). The skin first turns pale and then bright red. Frostbite can be painful, so handle with care.

The affected areas should be warmed with moist heat, which will help to restore circulation. Frequently, the skin may turn very dark, which means the tissue is dead. If damage from frostbite is severe, part of the tail or ear tips may actually fall off. Frostbite should be treated by a professional immediately.

Hairball

Cats are fastidious, and this often causes a hairball problem. Cats groom themselves by licking their fur. The cat's tongue feels rather like sandpaper to the touch because of its many small barbs. These barbs catch the hair as the cat licks itself, and the hair is swallowed. If enough hair collects in the stomach without passing into the intestinal tract, the cat will vomit in an effort to rid itself of it. A successfully vomited hairball often looks like a long cigar. If there is more hair than can be brought up, the cat will vomit its food, because there is no room for it in the stomach. These cats act normally, are hungry, and may try to eat the vomited food.

Treatment is aimed at eliminating the hair from the stomach by coating the stomach so the hair will pass into the intestine and the stool. White petroleum jelly (Vaseline®) is an excellent coating substance. Some cats like the taste and will lick it right off the spoon. It is also easily administered by placing one or two teaspoons on the mouth and paws; the cat will lick it off.

Treatment should be repeated daily until the petroleum jelly and hair are passed in the stool and the vomiting stops. It is important to realize that if the cat is depressed and not interested in food, or if the vomiting continues for more than two or three days, the problem is probably not hairballs. Veterinary attention should be sought as soon as possible.

Heart Disease

Heart disease is manifested in many ways. There are congenital heart problems; i.e., those that the cat is born with such as septal wall defects, valve defects, and aortic and pulmonary vessel defects. There are also the acquired heart diseases such as valve diseases, which cause the valves to thicken so they don't close completely, thus allowing blood to leak when a valve closes.

One frequent cause of valve problems is endocarditis, or infection of the valves. Antibiotics are often curative but damage is not reversible. Another group of acquired heart diseases is the myocardial diseases; i.e., diseases that affect the heart muscle. There are few diseases that cause a seemingly healthy cat to suddenly be on death's doorstep. Cardiomyopathy, or heart muscle disease, is one of these diseases. Cardiomyopathies can be divided into three major types:

The dilated cardiomyopathy is recognized by enlargement and dilation of all heart chambers. Recently, the deficiency of essential amino acid taurine has been incriminated as the cause of this deadly disease. As a result of this determination, cat food manufacturers have added additional taurine to cat food to prevent this disease.

The hypertrophic cardiomyopathy is the most common form of acquired heart disease. It is recognized by thickening of the muscles of the heart so that the chambers are very small. Embolisms (blood clots) are more frequent in this type of heart disease due to the improper pumping of blood. Signs of this disease are often acute and include labored breathing, depression, and paralysis or lameness of rear leg(s) due to a blood clot leaving the diseased heart, traveling down the aorta, and lodging at the division of the aorta to the vessels of the back legs. Treatment of this form of cardiomyopathy is limited to aspirin every third day and drugs to affect the force of heart contractions.

The restrictive form of cardiomyopathy is caused by fibrous tissue covering the heart muscles and restricting its movement. Although not as common as the other forms of cardiomyopathy, it is much more difficult to control.

All of the cardiomyopathies are serious heart diseases. Veterinarians are learning more each year as to the causes. As more knowledge is gained, better treatments will become available.

Heatstroke

Heatstroke is caused by the inability of the body to maintain its normal temperature because of environmental heat. It is often caused by keeping a cat in a hot area without adequate ventilation. Prompt treatment is urgent. Body temperature often gets as high as 107°F/41.5°C, and without quick cooling brain damage and death will occur.

Your first goal is to cool the body by immersing the cat in a cold water bath or running a garden hose on the body; either treatment is to be continued for at least 30 minutes. Then apply ice packs to the head, and keep them in place while transporting the cat to a veterinarian.

Heatstroke can be prevented by making sure your cat has plenty of shade and ventilation. If you must take your cat driving with you, park in the shade and leave all the windows partially open.

Poisoning

Cats are curious and like to investigate, which leads to many accidental poisonings. Often a cat will find an open can or bottle of chemical and knock it over. Naturally, the chemical gets on its fur and paws, and while licking the area clean, it swallows the possibly toxic substance. It is your responsibility to keep all potentially toxic products tightly closed and out of reach of your cat.

Poisoning symptoms are many and varied, and the toxic substance can be swallowed, absorbed through the skin, or inhaled. Basic emergency treatment for different poisons is as varied as the symptoms, so try to determine the poisoning agent. This is important, because what is correct first aid for one is the wrong treatment for another.

For instance, if the poisoning agent is a corrosive or a petroleum product, you want to forestall vomiting, since the returning chemical will cause further irritation and more severe burns. By giving your cat olive oil or egg whites, you are attempting to bind, or tie up, the chemical so it will not be absorbed.

However, if the chemical is not a corrosive or petroleum product, vomiting should be induced in order to empty the stomach of the poison. Of course, it is unlikely that you will see the poison being swallowed, so in either case, professional help should be sought immediately. If the cat has vomited, the material should be taken with you to the veterinarian for analysis. He or she will also want you to bring the suspected poison container, as this will be of prime importance in determining the most effective treatment.

It is appropriate to mention here the existence of human Poison Control Centers located all over the United States and in Canada. The National Animal Poison Control Center located in Urbana, Illinois, is the only center equipped to handle animal poisoning. This center can be reached by phoning 1-800-548-2423 anytime during the day or night. A fee for this service is required.

In addition to the obvious poisoning agents, ornamental houseplants can also be dangerous to a cat. It is safe to assume that all common houseplants are toxic to some degree, some more than others.

The best solution is to place the plants in areas where your cat cannot reach them, and use hanging baskets for the more toxic types. If in doubt, call and ask the vet if the type of plant you have or are going to purchase could harm your cat. The vet will tell you whether or not it poses a hazard.

Smoke inhalation from fires is another possible threat to cats. Do not risk your own life to save your cat. Leave that task to the firefighters or those trained in rescue. If your cat does suffer from smoke inhalation, get it away from the area and into fresh air. If it is conscious, flush the eyes with diluted boric acid solution or plain water to wash out soot and other particles.

If the animal is not breathing or if the heart is not beating, use artificial respiration and/or CPR. If the smoke is intense, the airway and lungs may also be seriously damaged by inhalation of smoke and heated air. Burned lungs collect fluid, causing shortness of breath. To ease breathing, the cat's head should be kept higher than its body. Also, a burned airway may swell shut; it is imperative to keep this airway open. Immediate professional help is essential.

Carbon monoxide poisoning can be caused by faulty heaters, but it is often due to our own carelessness. Cats often suffer carbon monoxide poisoning from being transported in car trunks. This is dangerous and inhumane.

Characteristic signs are depression, lack of coordination, heavy panting, deep red gums, and possibly convulsions. Oxygen is needed immediately, and the cat should be taken to a veterinarian at once. If there is no heartbeat or respiration, CPR is essential.

Puncture Wound

A puncture wound may be difficult to see because it is often covered with hair. The first sign may be a limp if it is on the leg, or slightly blood-tinged fur on other parts of the body.

If the puncture wound is on the body, you can see the extent of the injury more clearly after you have clipped the hair around the area. After cleaning the wound with 3% hydrogen peroxide, examine for an imbedded foreign object, such as a splinter or shard of glass, and remove it if possible. Puncture wounds are deceptive; they can be deeper than they look. These deep wounds often damage muscle tissue, causing fluid to accumulate. It is best to leave the wound open so it can drain.

An exception to leaving the wound open would be excessive bleeding or a chest wound. Chest wounds can be very serious. If there is a hole through the entire chest wall, a "sucking" noise will be heard as the cat breathes. The act of breathing causes outside air to rush into the chest and around the lungs, causing lung collapse.

Your first priority is to seal the hole quickly to keep air from entering. If a foreign object such as a stick or an arrow is in the chest, do not attempt to pull it out. This could open the hole and lead to lung collapse. Just bandage tightly around the object and take the cat to the vet immediately.

Shock

Shock is extremely serious—the No. 1 killer in accidents. It is a reaction to heavy internal or external bleeding, or any serious injury that "scares" the body; for example, a large wound or amputation with heavy blood loss.

To compensate for the loss, the heart beats faster; this keeps the blood pressure from falling. The blood vessels that supply the outside of the body narrow. This conserves blood so that vital organs of the body continue to receive their normal blood supply.

However, if there is heavy blood loss or other serious injury, the body overreacts and causes a pooling of blood in the internal organs. This can cause death due to a drop in external blood pressure and possible oxygen starvation of the brain. Pale gums or cold extremities indicate shock.

When shock is present, you want to reverse the process. Elevate the hindquarters to allow more blood to reach the brain. Stop visible bleeding to prevent a drop in blood pressure. Wrap the cat in a blanket with hot water bottles to help keep the body temperature up. This is necessary because the external blood vessels become constricted, and the outside of the body becomes very cold due to lack of normal blood flow. Raising the temperature of the outside of the body helps conserve heat.

Treatment for shock cannot hurt your cat and may save its life. The victim should be taken to the veterinarian immediately.

Swallowing Thread, String, Or Yarn

Cats that play with thread, string, or yarn are bound to swallow some sooner or later. A long piece of thread, string, or yarn, if swallowed, can cause a blockage of the intestinal tract with subsequent perforation. This needs immediate surgical intervention. Sometimes you can catch the cat swallowing the material. If so, give petroleum jelly immediately by rubbing small amounts on the mouth and paws so it can be licked off. Hopefully, this will ease the passage of the material. More often, we don't see the cat swallow the material, and all we see is a piece hanging out of the mouth or rectum. Never pull too hard, and if you get resistance, you should stop and cut off the material as short as possible and then follow with petroleum jelly. Never use mineral oil or any other oil.

Vets often find cats have swallowed thread with a needle attached. Sometimes the needle ends up in the stomach and must be removed surgically. At other times, the needle gets caught in the throat or roof of the mouth. This will be evidenced by the cat choking and pawing at its mouth.

If a cat swallows thread, string, or yarn and begins to vomit, a vet should be seen immediately. The best treatment is prevention; don't permit the cat access to thread, string, or yarn.

Unconsciousness

If the cat is unconscious, it is important to check its vital signs immediately. Is it breathing? Watch its chest for movement. If the cat is not breathing, artificial respiration must be performed.

Is the heart beating? If not, perform CPR (cardiopulmonary resuscitation). This is a combination of artificial respiration and cardiac massage. It may take time. It should be continued until the cat is breathing well by itself, or until you can get it to a veterinarian. It should be continued on the way. Your continued efforts may save the cat's life.

If the cat is not breathing and/or the heart is not beating, before starting treatment make sure the airway is clear. Remove any foreign material and extend the neck so the cat will be able to breathe. Your first priority is to get the heart beating and the cat breathing.

Watch for shock. In shock cases, the circulation to the external parts of the body is greatly diminished. Examine the gums and the inside of the upper lip. If white or very pale, shock is almost certainly present. Start treatment immediately. Shock is the No. 1 killer in accidents.

Vomiting

Vomiting is one of the most commonly encountered problems in veterinary medicine. It is nature's way of permitting the animal to rid its stomach of irritating substances such as spoiled food or other foreign material such as hairballs or plants. But not all vomiting is due to simple irritation.

More serious causes are viral infections, obstructions caused by string or other foreign objects, and diseases of the liver, pancreas, or kidney. Initial home treatment should be conservative, following the steps on page 194. However, it is important to seek professional help if there are signs of bleeding, or if the cat is depressed and still vomiting after initial efforts at control have failed.

FIRST AID SUPPLIES FOR YOUR CAT

Rectal thermometer

Cotton-tipped swabs—for cleaning the ears

Mineral oil and eyedropper—for use at bath time

Cat nail clippers, slicker brush, and cat comb for grooming

Styptic powder—to stop bleeding from a nail

Eye wash

3% hydrogen peroxide—this is a must for cleaning wounds

Antibacterial skin ointment—e.g. Bacitracin

Kaopectate® for treatment of diarrhea

Pepto-Bismol® for treatment of vomiting

Petroleum jelly—for treatment of hairballs

Plastic or nylon eyedropper or dose syringe for giving liquid medication

Scissors

Tweezers

Adhesive tape, 1-inch and 2-inch rolls

Gauze bandage, 1-inch and 2-inch rolls

Sterile gauze pads

Triangular bandage and safety pins (for holding dressings in place)

Blanket—for use in treatment for shock or as a stretcher

2-inch and 3-inch strips of clean cloth, 2-4 feet long—to tie an injured cat to a board stretcher

Wooden rule or tongue depressor for use with a tourniquet

Wooden paint mixing sticks and cotton batting for splints

Ice bags or chemical ice pack—for use in cases of heat prostration or burns

Index

Index

Index